MILES ◆ INTERNATIONAL
Sponsorship Education

Double Money Back Guarantee

After purchasing Sponsorship Recruitment 101-102, participants who have actively used and followed our Systems Approach for 12-months and have not secured at least $5,000 in cash, products or services will be entitled to a double refund.

Read just a few comments from professionals like yourself who have used our program:

"Outstanding course! This information will help increase our funding by 60%!"

--Charles C. Achane
President
Imperial Calcasieu RC & D

James 1:5 says "whomever lacks wisdom he should ask...and GOD will grant it to him abundantly." This program was the answer to my prayers! God bless."

--Rev. James Barker
First Baptist Church
Jacksonville Florida

"This course made me focus on targeted sponsors. I took lots of notes and have a plan of action ready to go."

--Denise Scarborough
Membership Coordinator
Greater Lafayette Chamber of Commerce

"A lot of information for the price."

--Sammye Meadows
Executive Director
Vail Alpine Garden Foundation

"This course really makes you focus on sponsor benefits and gets the creative juices flowing."

--Alastair Lyall
Special Events Coordinator
City of Avon

"This course is excellent for not-for-profit fund-raisers or beginners."

--Amy Capra
Special Events Coordinator
Denver Botanic Gardens

"Your systematic approach provides a powerful mechanism for creating successful continuing corporate partnerships."

--Annabel Brooks,
Director of Public Relations
St. Johns River Community College

"I've increased my knowledge by 100%."

--John Jackson, Director
St. Cloud Parks & Recreation

This course was a valuable tool for securing more funds in this day and age of shrinking government support. Excellent course!"

--Marcia S. Breiter
Program Coordinator
City of Miami

"Anthony exudes tremendous passion for not-for-profits, one of the best I have ever seen."

--Susan Cantiberos
Program Administrator
City of Bellevue

BRING THIS SEMINAR TO YOUR AREA

We can customize this program and present to your group (large or small) at a time and location that is convenient. We also provide FREE consultation. For details e-mail us at: anthony@MilesInternational.org

Requests for such permission should be addressed to:

MILES INTERNATIONAL
5012 Erringer Place
Philadelphia, PA 19144 USA
Phone: 1- (215) 843-0571
Fax: 1- (215) 843-0572

Printed in The United States of America

This publication is designed to provide accurate and authoritative information in regard to the subject matter covered. It is sold with the understanding that the publisher is not engaged in rendering legal, accounting, or other professional service. If legal advice or other expert assistance is required, the services of Anthony Miles should be sought.

Cover Design: Josh Laird
Text Layout: Renee D. Crenshaw

ABOUT THE AUTHOR

Anthony "The Money Man" Miles is one of the world's leading authorities in Corporate Sponsorships and Promotional Activities. He has established himself at an early age as a developer of creative marketing & promotions strategies. His marketing skills coupled with his knowledge of consumer trends, grass-roots branding and strategic partnerships makes Anthony one of the most sought after speakers and sponsorship improvement consultants in North America.

The diversity of his work is reflected in the variety of people he has helped, including actor Danny Glover, comedian Tommy Davidson; recording artists Boyz II Men and NAJEE; as well as organizations such as NIKE, Thomas Kemper, First Interstate Bank and Power Bar. His seminars and manuals have made a profound impact on thousands of properties throughout North America...from the American Red Cross...to Universities...to Sports Commissions...to Symphonies...to Parks & Rec...to Association Executives...to Professional Golf...and various Cities in the United States.

An entrepreneur, Anthony has founded seven companies in industries as varied as business development to a clothing line for affluent consumers. He is the author of three marketing related titles: **Sponsorship Recruitment 101-102**, **How To Produce Millions In Corporate Sponsorship** and **What Every Agent & Celebrity Needs To Know**. He is the producer of the best selling not-for-profit sponsorship seminar of all time, Sponsorship Recruitment 101-102, thousands have attended his live events. Anthony has a burning desire to share his sponsorship performance changing ideas, strategies, principles, concepts, and techniques with as many people as possible, so he created the Sponsorship Recruitment 101-102 manual in 1993. Using his knowledge gained from interacting with properties from every denomination, he made it more powerful with the **How To Produce Millions In Corporate Sponsorship System.**

He is the recipient of over 50 community service, business and leadership awards. Anthony has earned his professional reputation the right way, though dedication, customer satisfaction and just plan hard work. He has dedicated his life to helping individuals and organizations meet their funding objectives. This passion has earned him the nickname **"The Money Man."**

Many people throughout North America feel Anthony is the most dynamic, most charismatic sponsorship speaker on the circuit today. His ability to electrify a crowd with his presence as well as his cutting-edge strategies have put him into a class of his own. Simply put, Anthony is the **Michael Jordan** of the not-for-profit sponsorship world.

Anthony lives in Bainbridge Island, Washington and Philadelphia, PA. He is the father of two children.

Acknowledgments

My thanks to the many people, who in different ways, have helped me develop the knowledge and gain the experience to deliver the most affordable and comprehensive sponsorship book on the market.

To my creator and the lord of my life for shaping my destiny. To my parents who encouraged me to recognize and pursue what I really wanted out of life. To William Ellerbee for being a lifelong inspiration and to Melvin Wingate for using sports to teach me what it takes to go the extra mile, which I have used consistently to a accomplish all my goals.

To Tom McClure who taught me the ropes on how-to write winning proposals for government and commercial solicitations. To Jim Thomas and Josephus Lewis, who were there during the tough nonprofit fundraising days to talk, listen, laugh, and give sound advice. To Marion Britain at the chamber who helped me launch my sponsorship career by hosting my first seminar. To the Leadership Kitsap Board of Directors for identifying me as an emerging leader and selecting me in the inaugural class.

To my fellow Rotarians who grounded me in areas of economic development, politics, and public speaking. To Chuck Huddleston, Will & Renee Witt, Dr. Eugene Hertzke, Dr. Patrick Bays, Karen Williams, Ed Cruz, Peter Crane and Anthony Flow who invested in my entertainment venture.

To all the people who have attended my workshops, speeches and seminars who encouraged me to be candid and who continuously let me know how timely and useful my techniques and strategies are.

To contributors Renee D. Crenshaw and Marcus Miles for believing in me, and the importance of this information. To Vanessa Miles for her contribution to this book.

Finally, to Linda, Nicholas and Alexis Miles who supported me while I spent countless hours away from home to perfect my craft, without you none of this would be possible.

TABLE OF CONTENTS

<u>MODULE 13.</u>   <u>SPONSORSHIP RESOURCES</u>

13.1 Eight-week Fast Track Sponsorship Course
13.2 Regional Sponsorship Course
13.3 6-month Coaching Program

Introduction

Many properties are quickly discovering corporations are willing to pay billions (cash, products and services) in-exchange for marketing links. With virtually all properties facing tough budget times it's immoral to fail to learn exactly how-to secure sponsors to produce additional funding. Now imagine your property receiving millions of dollars every year - with each deal containing cash, products or services.

You may wonder whether it is at all possible for your property to achieve this delightful and profitable experience. Yes, you are no different from the countless other properties who started from scratch and who are now producing incredible results.

If it's as simple as all that, then why doesn't every property secure millions in sponsorship revenue? That's the $64,000 question which this manual will try to answer for you. The author draws on 10 years of experience to tell you what to and what not to do. You should be able to steer a straight course and eliminate guesswork, because a workable plan will be provided.

Much of your success depends on you - how you follow the rules and how you apply the knowledge you gain as you proceed. This manual shall define in simple language all the essential ingredients that help to make a smooth-running sponsorship program. While the manual provides the recipe, you in turn will be the chef to carry it out. Two bakers given the same recipe rarely produce the same results. Personal considerations enter into this undertaking. Pardon the pun, but we hope you have what it takes to produce the "dough" you are after. Undoubtedly you have the interest and ability; otherwise, you would not be seeking help.

Here Are Some Of The Things You'll Learn And Gain From The *How To Produce Millions In Corporate Sponsorship System:*

11 characteristics of million dollar sponsorship producers.
Thinking about becoming a million dollar sponsorship producer? Or want to get to the $1,000,000 threshold faster? Either way, this is the information for you! Anthony identifies the crucial traits, the "megatraits" that produce million dollar sponsorship practitioners. Must reading if you want to join the club.

Why most properties never meet their funding objectives ... and what you should do so you will. Most properties selling sponsorships are "winging it" with predictable results. This is immoral when corporations are willing to pay billions in-exchange for marketing links. Anthony shows you why most properties fail to meet their funding objectives...and provides specific steps to follow so they will.

Why you need a sponsorship plan, why you resist creating one.
Makes a clear case why every property needs a functional sponsorship plan to succeed, how to overcome your resistance to creating one, and what should go in it. A must, particularly for new and struggling sponsorship programs.

How to stay ahead of the competition-all the time.
Provides the details you need to stay ahead of your competitors all the time... and use over 500 emerging and active sponsorship categories to outmaneuver them. Crucial facts if you want to win the competitor's race.

What every property absolutely MUST do before contacting any sponsor.
Anthony talks about precisely what you have to do before you present your property to any sponsor so that you identify all of your salable assets.

How to find out exactly what a sponsor wants...so you can give it to them.
In this module, Anthony helps people who hate making cold calls... and cannot figure out how to get sponsors to tell them what benefits they want. If you can solve this problem, you can sell any proposal. Here are the guidelines you need to create a client centered prospecting letter...and how to use it. When you do, your prospects start telling you precisely what they want...all you have to do is give it to them to close the deal.

Why you can't just mail your way to sponsorship millions...what you should be doing instead.
Plenty of sponsorship 'gurus' in not-for-profits think they can just mail generic proposals and build a million dollar sponsorship program. As Anthony points out, that's just a lot of hooey! Properties who just mail generic proposals have a terrifying high failure rate. Anthony points out why, and suggests a specific alternative that makes economic sense.

Your worst fears realized, or what to do when a corporation declines your proposal.
The competition for corporate sponsorship dollars for not-for-profits has never been greater and will get worse. You can count on getting turned down, often. What you do next determines whether your organization will ever get the money it needs from these marketing driven funding sources. Here are Anthony's guidelines for turning a no into a yes, for doing what it takes to build a win-win relationship with this funding source. Since this will happen to you (if it is not happening already), prepare for it now.

The Top 5 sales-killing mistakes you are making...and how to avoid them.
Anthony interviews Marcus Miles, the super-smart sales and customer service guru, about the 5 biggest mistakes' people make in **TELESPONSORSALES**, **PRESENTATIONS** and **DURING THE PARTNERSHIP** that kill the deal, and how to avoid them. Must reading if you're trying to sell regional and national sponsorships from a local market

How to make sure your sponsors get the maximum return on their investment.

This isn't a module about collecting you cash…it's about how to connect with your sponsors products or services so that it effectively reaches your demographic segment. Here is what you got to do to achieve this crucial objective.

6 practical exercises to create your plan of action.

Many sponsorship consultants have sprung up charging as much as $7,000 for providing this kind of advice. Anthony provides a systematic approach with worksheets you can use to: identify your salable assets, price your salable assets, survey prospects, formulate a budget, create your property plan, and prepare customized proposals. Why pay 7G's when Anthony provides these steps right here?

How to get Anthony to help you produce millions.

Whether you're starting out or you've been soliciting sponsors for awhile, you face new challenges and questions daily. Where can you turn for sound advice and candid answers? Our newest resource tool, Technical Support serves as part therapist, coach and expert resource. It's like having a dedicated sponsorship staff member on call. How many other companies offer this kind of customer support?

Many questions that you have in mind will be answered. If after a careful reading of this manual, you still seek answers to your sponsorship problems, you are invited to write the author at International Money Group where he serves as sponsorship trainer and performance consultant.

ANTHONY B. MILES

MILES INTERNATIONAL
5012 Erringer Place
Philadelphia, PA 19144 USA

The most comprehensive and affordable, step-b-step sponsorship recruitment training program on the market!

Sponsorship Recruitment 101-102™
Self-Study Course

Module One

UNDERSTANDING THE GAME OF SPONSORSHIP

Understanding The Game Of Sponsorship

Anthony B. Miles

With Renee Crenshaw

1.0   Understanding The Game of Sponsorship

Sponsorship has become a major source of funding for local and international events involving sports, the arts, the environment, media, community projects, education and various other properties. The value of sponsorship has increased in the last five to ten years, more and more corporations have added sponsorship to their marketing mix.

These corporations recognize that well-constructed sponsorships can provide highly effective ways to present corporate messages - whether the message is primarily a sales/marketing one or a community relations one. So where do properties begin? Any property interested in investigating sponsorship should begin by understanding the game.

The purpose of this module is to help you enter this industry with open eyes. What is the industry terminology? How are sponsorships structured? What benefits do I have to offer? We will cover all of this and more in this foundation building module.

1.1   Sponsorship Marketing

Sponsorship marketing is where a corporation sell its product by "piggy backing" its advertisement on a property. "Let's say Blue Cross/Blue Shield thinks your audience demographics matches theirs. Let's form a partnership? What do you say"? The purpose of this manual is to help you get to the point where ultimately you do say yes, but not until after a great deal of negotiating and discussion of terms. Whether you are being forced into sponsorship because of current budget constraints or interest in the industry is really not the issue. To stay competitive you must make sponsorship work for yourself, sponsor and your audience without compromising your mission.

Sponsorship Defined
Sponsorship is any communication by which the sponsor, for the mutual benefit of the sponsor and the sponsored party, contractually provides <u>cash</u>, <u>products</u> or <u>services</u> in order to provide a positive relationship between the sponsor's image, brands, products or services and the sponsored event, activity, organization or individual.

Rules of Selling Sponsorship
For the most part, selling sponsorship used to go like this: You would base your fee on your need or desire, then try to justify it to sponsors. The sponsors in the absence of an industry standard for valuing sponsorship, would automatically question your fee and counter with a rock bottom offer or no offer. Negotiating (if it took place at all) focused on price and away from content.

The trick now is to:

- Move the focus of your pitch from price to your demographics
- Identify overlooked benefits-tangible and intangible
    1. Tangible benefits - these include things like program book acknowledgment, on-site signage, sampling and hospitality
    2. Intangible benefits - these include audience loyalty and category exclusivity.
- Address sponsor communication needs. What message are they trying to convey.
- Enhance your credibility. Give success stories to potential sponsors.

1.2   Sponsorship vs. Philanthropy

All properties seeking sponsorship had best understand which corporate purse they're looking to. The request for donations is vastly different from a sponsorship relationship. For example:

- The contact point is different;
- The goals are different; and
- The language is different.

The following chart is a starting point for properties:

Sponsorship	Philanthropy
Definition: any communication by which the sponsor, for the mutual benefit of sponsor and sponsored party, contractually provides cash, products or services in order to provide a positive relationship between the sponsor's image, brands, products or services and a sponsored event, activity, organization or individual	donations that are typically caused related
Publicity: Highly public	Usually little widespread fanfare
Source: Typically from marketing, advertising, or communications budgets	From charitable donations or philanthropy budgets.
Accounting: Written off as a full business expense, like promotional printing expense or media placement	Writeoff is limited to 75% of net income. This limit was increased from 20% earlier this year. As a result, accounting/tax considerations are less likely to influence the way a corporation designates funding of a not-for-profit organization.
Objectives: To sell more products/services	To be a good corporate citizen; to enhance the corporate image with closet stakeholders (i.e. employees, shareholders, suppliers)
Partner/Recipient: events; teams; arts or cultural organizations, projects, causes and programs	Larger donations are typically cause related (education, health, diseases, disasters, and environmental), but can also be cultural, artistic, or sports related. At times funding is specifically designated for a project or program; at times it is provided for operating budgets.

1.3   Sponsorship Language

Here are 45 key sponsorship related terms you should know. Each term will be used repeatedly throughout this manual. Over time you must incorporate these terms in all your communications to ensure effective dialogue with sponsorship prospects.

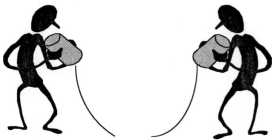

1. ADVERTISING: Non-personal promotion of your product, service or company in mass media that is openly paid for and/or sponsored by you.

2. ADVERTORIAL: A print advertisement which is styled to resemble the editorial format and type face of the publication in which it runs. Most publishers require advertorials to be labeled "advertisements" at the top.

3. ANNOUNCEMENT: An advertising message in broadcast media, commonly 10, 15, 30, or 60 seconds in length. Synonymous with "commercial" and usually referred to as a "spot."

4. AUDIENCE: The public, individuals, or organizations to which the sponsorship is directed.

5. AWARENESS LEVEL: The percentage of the target market that knows about the existence of your products, services or company.

6. BANNERS: Signage provided as temporary acknowledgment.

7. BENEFITS: The rewards to be realized from the use of the product or service.

8. BUYING INFLUENCES: All the individuals who have a say in the decision or the selection of a product or service.

9. CATEGORY EXCLUSIVITY: Rights of a sponsor to be recognized as the only company, product or service associated with the sponsorship opportunity.

10. COLUMN INCHES: An ad one inch high and one column wide is exactly one column inch in size.

11. COMPETITIVE PRICING STRATEGY: Sponsorship package is presented at market value but offered to sponsor at a lower rate.

12. COST-PLUS PRICING STRATEGY: Calculate the actual cost of the sponsorship package and then a present percentage is added.

13. DEMOGRAPHICS: The population and makeup of your audience.

14. END-USER: The individual or company who is the final purchaser of the product or service.

15. FAMILIARITY: Although not used in this manual, this term refers to the perception of individuals who have had actual experiences with your product or service.

16. FEATURES: Physical description of the attributes of a product or service; these are different from benefits.

17. FREQUENCY: The number of times you hit the average person with your advertising campaign.

18. LEAD GENERATION: Methods by which prospects are identified.

19. LOTTERIES: Games of chance that involve an entry fee.

20. MEDIA INVOLVEMENT: A method of describing a purchase decision-making influence on the basis of reading, viewing and listening habits.

21. MEDIUM: What is used to reach consumers (television, radio and newspapers).

22. METHOD OF DISTRIBUTION: How the product or service is brought into contact with the prospect for evaluation and/or purchase.

23. PATRONAGE: No commercial advantage is sought in return for support.

24. PERCEPTION: The impression most commonly held by your target market about your product, service or company. Perceptions may not necessarily reflect reality.

25. POSITIONING: The renting of a place in the mind of the marketplace for your product or service with regard to your competition.

26. PROMOTIONAL CONSIDERATION: Cash, product or service fee.

27. PROCESS OF INFLUENCE: How the sponsorship media publicity message influences its target audience.

28. PRODUCT SAMPLING: The sponsor is entitled to a product sampling station.

29. PRIMARY MARKET RESEARCH: This is the only true, measurable way to determine awareness, perception, and purchase decision making-factors as they relate to your product or service. Ideal for identifying marketing problems and to establish a basis of comparison to analyze the effectiveness of a communication program.

30. PRODUCT LIFE CYCLE: The stages through which your product's life passes, including: introductory, acceptance, maturity and decline.

31. PROMOTION: That part of the marketing mix which relates to creating awareness, effecting perception and consummating the sale of your product or service; includes both personal and non-personal.

32. PULL: A marketing strategy that calls for end-user demand to be created in order to convince pipeline influences to carry/represent your product or service.

33. PUSH: A marketing strategy that calls for pipeline influences to promote your product or service.

34. REACH: Number of people who read, listen or watch.

35. RELATIVE VALUE PRICING: Pricing strategies based on what the managers think the market will bear.

36. REMOTE: A promotion where the radio disc jockey comes to your place of business and does a live broadcast.

37. RIGHT OF FIRST REFUSAL: Right to have the first opportunity to purchase something, such as the right to sponsor an opportunity, when those sponsorship rights become available; the rights to meet the terms of any offer received for such sponsorship rights.

38. SHARE OF MARKET: The percentage of the overall market's expenditure for a product or service garnered by your (or a competitor's) product or service.

39. SIGNAGE: Banners, scorecards, flags, decals containing the sponsor's identification.

40. SPONSOR: Any corporation or legal person providing financial or other sponsored support.

41. SPONSORED PARTY: Any individual or legal person receiving direct or indirect support from a sponsor in relation with an activity or event.

42. SPONSORSHIP: Any communication by which the sponsor, for the mutual benefit of sponsor and sponsored party, contractually provides cash, products or services in order to provide a positive relationship between the sponsor's image, brands, products or services and a sponsored event, activity, organization or individual.

43. SPOT: The industry name for a radio commercial.

44. SWEEPSTAKES: These are games of chance that make it clear that there is no purchase required. These are the most common promotions.

45. TITLE SPONSOR: The sponsor whose name is part of the sponsorship opportunity.

1.4 Sponsorship Motives

Do you have a particular corporation you wish to approach about sponsorship? I have learned as a practitioner that to be effective you have to understand both the motive and objectives of the specific corporation you are recruiting.

Motives

Contrary to what we would believe, corporations seldom, if ever sponsor for purely altruistic reasons. To approach a corporation because you think you have a good cause is naïve. Let me make you aware of some of the motives of corporate sponsorship. As you begin to understand their motives, you can better present your property so their motives are met and fulfilled.

MOTIVE #1: ENHANCED AWARENESS & ATTITUDES
- Public & community relations (charity tie-in)
- Bring company within public focus at grass root level
- Media exposure

MOTIVE #2: IMAGE ENHANCEMENT/LIFESTYLE ASSOCIATION
- Have sponsorship opportunity prestige rub off on their image as a company

MOTIVE #3: BRAND VALUES/POSITIONING
- On-site exposure
- Dual name reinforcement with sponsorship opportunity
- Media acknowledgment and attention
- Sponsorship as a medium

MOTIVE #4: TRADE RELATIONS/STRATEGIC ALLIANCES
- Entertain current and future clients
- Facilitate cross promotions with other partners
- Share the sponsorship relationship with accounts and vendors to enhance future negotiations
- Positioning the company as the best in the industry (market dominance)
- Build continuing partnerships through active employee involvement

MOTIVE #5: DIFFERENTIATION FROM COMPETITOR
- Category exclusivity
- Target marketing

MOTIVE #6: SALES
- Brand and service loyalty
- Use the sponsorship as a rallying point for vendor sales incentive programs
- Sales promotions
- Sampling
- Merchandising
- Increased retail space
- Income generating extensions: Charity tie-in

Now that you have an idea of common motives of sponsors, commit these to memory and listen carefully during the recruitment process (explained in module 6) and hone in on the motives that's important to each individual sponsor. Be prepared to emphasize these in your proposal. Listen very carefully in the early stages of research because most sponsors will communicate them to you. Be sure to pick up on these and be prepared to illustrate that your property has the assets to meet their motives.

1.5 Sponsorship Categories

Categories provide exclusivity or prominence associated with a product or service. Every potential sponsor falls into one of these categories, and that means there are endless opportunities to obtain marketing driven funding sources.

Product Category Index

Academies
Accessories
Acids
Adding Machines
Addressing Machines
Adhesive Plasters
Adhesive Tapes
Advertising Novelties
Aerosols
Air Brakes
Air Conditioners
Air Rifles
Airline
Alcohol, Anti-freeze
Alcohol, Medical
Alcohol, Beverage
Ale
Aluminum
Ammunition
Amplifiers
Amusement Parks
Amusements
Antennas
Antiques
Antiseptics
Art Galleries
Art Glass
Art Objects
Artificial Flowers
Athletic Shoes
Audio Equipment
Automobile Rental
Automobile Tires
Automobiles
Automotive Parts
Automotive Repair Centers
Axles

B

Baby Carriages
Bags, Leather
Bags, Paper
Baking Products
Bandages

Baseballs
Basketballs
Baskets
Bathroom Equipment
Batteries, Auto
Bearings
Bedding
Beds
Belting, Machinery
Belts
Beverages
Bicycles
Billiard Tables
Bindings, Cloth
Binoculars
Bird Supplies
Biscuits
Bitters
Blankets
Bleach
Blinds
Blouses
Bluing
Boats
Boilers, House
Boilers, Machinery
Bolts
Bonds (Surety)
Book Cases
Bookkeeping Machines
Books
Boots
Bowling Centers
Boxes
Braces
Brake Linings
Brass Equipment
Breakfast Food
Brick
Broadcasting
Brokers, Insurance
Brooms

Product Category Index

Brushes, House
Brushes, Paint
Buckets
Building Materials
Bulbs, Plants
Burglar Alarms
Burial Vaults
Bus Lines
Butter

C

Cable Television
Cakes
Calculators
Cameras
Camping Equipment
Camps
Candles
Candy
Canned Goods
Canoes
Cans
Canvas
Car Rental
Carbon Paper
Carburetor
Cardboard
Carpet Sweepers
Carpets
Cartons
Cash Registers
Casters
Cat Food
Catalog Stores
Cattle
Cedar Chests
Cement
Cereals
Chains
Chainsaw

Chambers of Commerce
Champagne
Cheese
Chemicals , Industrial
Chemicals, Medical
Chewing Gum
Children's Wear
China
Chlorides
Chocolate

Church Supplies
Cigarette Cases
Cigars
Citizen Band Radios
Civic Organizations
Cleansers
Clocks
Cloth
Clothes Dryers
Clothing, Boy's
Clothing, Girl's
Clothing, Men's
Clothing, Women's
Cocoa
Coffee
Coffee Brewing Equipment
Coins
Collections Agencies
Colleges
Colors, paint
Combs
Commercial Trailers
Commissions
Communications Systems
Computers
Condensed Milk
Condiments
Confectionery
Construction, Building
Consultants
Contact Lenses
Contractors, Building
Controlling Instruments
Convection Ovens
Cookies
Cooking Utensils
Cooperatives
Copiers
Cordage
Cordials
Corn Plasters
Correspondence Schools
Corrugated Material
Cosmetics
Cough Syrups
Councils
Crackers
Crafts
Cream, Skin
Cream Separators

Product Category Index

Product Category Index

Gloves
Glue
Golf Supplies
Graphites
Grates
Greases
Greeting Cards
Grocers
Guilds
Guitars
Gum, Chewing
Guns

H

HMO
Hair Care Products
Hair Dressers
Handbags
Handkerchiefs
Handling Equipment
Hardware
Harnesses
Harps
Hats
Hay Balers
Health Foods
Health Supplies
Hearing Aids
Heaters, Kerosene
Heaters, Portable
Heating Appliances & Equipment
Heating Pads
Helicopters
Hobbies
Hose
Hosiery
Hospital Equipment
Hospitals
Hot Water Bags
Household Paper
Hunting Equipment

I

Ice Cream
Ignition Systems
Incubators
Infant Furniture
Infants Wear
Ink

Inner Tubes
Insecticides
Instant Coffee & Tea
Instant Printing Services
Institutions
Insurance
Iron
Irrigation Equipment

J

Jeans
Jewelry
Journals-Publisher

K

Kitchen Cabinets
Kitchen Utensils
Kites
Knives

L

Lace
Lacquers
Lamps, Electric
Lasers
Lawn Care
Lawn Mowers
Laxatives
Leather
Lenses, Optical
Libraries
Light Bulbs
Lighters, Cigar & Cigarette
Lighting Fixtures
Linens
Lingerie
Liqueurs
Liquor
Lithographers
Locks
Lotteries
Lubricants
Lubricating Systems
Luggage
Lumber
Lye

M

Machinery
Magazines
Mail Order
Mailing Lists
Malt

Product Category Index

Manicure Implements
Mantels
Marble

Margarine
Marine Engines
Marine Oil
Marketing Research
Marketing Services
Matches
Materials, Building
Materials, Machinery
Mattresses
Meals
Mechanical Toys
Medical Equipment
Memorials
Men's Furnishings
Metals
Microcomputers
Microwave Components
Microwave Ovens
Military Services
Milk
Mineral Waters
Mirrors
Missiles
Mixes - Cake, Biscuit, Etc.
Mobile Homes
Molded Rubber
Mopeds
Mops & Polishes
Mortgage Companies
Motion Picture Cameras
Motor Boats
Motor Oil
Motorcycles
Motors
Moving Companies
Mufflers, Automobiles
Museums
Music Publishers
Musical Instruments

N

Nails
Neckwear
Needles
Needlework
Newspapers

Nonprofit Membership Organizations
Notions
Novelties
Nursery Accessories, Garden
Nursery, Plants
Nursing Homes
Nuts, Edible

O

Office Furniture
Office Supplies
Oil Burners
Oil, Cooking
Oil Drilling Equipment
Oil Exploration
Oil, lubricating
Oil, Paint
Ointments
Optical Goods
Orchards
Organs
Orthopedic Appliances
Outdoor Advertising
Outdoor Furniture
Outing Supplies
Ovens
Oxygen Equipment

P

Paint Brushes
Painting Machines
Painting
Paints
Paper Boxes
Paper, Household
Paper, Industrial
Patterns
Pencils
Pens
Perennials
Perfumes
Periodicals
Pet Foods
Photo Finishing Services
Photo Supplies
Photocopy Equipment
Photographers
Pianos
Pictures
Pies
Pigments

Product Category Index

Pillow
Pins
Pipes, Smoking
Pistols
Piston Rings
Plants
Plastics
Playing Cards
Plows
Plumbing Fixtures
Pneumatic Tires
Polishes
Pollution Control Equipment
Pool Tables
Port Authorities
Pottery
Poultry Feeds & Equipment
Precious Stones
Precision Instruments
Prefabricated Buildings
Prefabricated Homes
Premiums
Preserves
Presses
Printing
Proprietary Medicines
Public Accountants
Public Service Companies
Publications
Pumps
Puzzles

R

Race Tracks
Radar Equipment
Radiators
Radio Parts
Radio Stations
Radios
Railroads
Railway Equipment
Razor Blades
Real Estate
Records, Phonograph
Refrigerators
Religious Broadcasting
Resins
Resorts
Restaurants
Ribbons, Typewriter

Rings
Robes
Roller Bearings
Roller Skates
Roofing
Rope
Rubber Goods, Medical
Rubber Heels
Rubber Molded Products
Rubber Stamps
Rum

S

Saddlery
Safes
Safety Razors
Sailboats
Sales Promotion Services
Salves
Sanitariums
Saws
Scales
School Supplies
Scientific Instruments
Scissors & Shears
Screens
Screws
Seat Covers
Securities
Seeding Machines
Seeds
Separators
Serums
Sewing Machine
Sewing Notions
Shades
Shaving Accessories
Sheets
Shingles
Shipping Companies
Shirts
Shock Absorbers
Shoe Fittings
Shoe Polish
Signs
Silverware
Skates
Skirts
Skis
Slate

Product Category Index

Sleds
Slip Covers
Slippers
Smoke Detectors
Snap Fasteners
Snowmobiles
Soap, Household
Soap, Toilet
Societies
Socks
Soft Drinks
Solvents
Soups
Space Vehicles
Spark Plugs
Spices
Spool Cotton
Sprayers
Spraying Compounds
Spring, Bed
Sprinklers
Stains, Paints
Stamps & Coins
Starch
Stationery
Steamship Lines
Steel
Stereo Equipment
Stock Brokers
Stock Feed
Stocks
Stokers
Stone
Storage
Store Equipment
Stoves
Street Maintenance Equipment
Sugar
Suitcases
Suits, men's
Suit, Women's
Sulphur
Supermarkets
Surf Boards
Surgical Instruments
Sweaters
Swimming Pools
Switches
Synthetics

Syringes
Syrups
Table Mats
Tables
Tacks
Talcum Powder
Tanners
Tape Recorders
Tea
Telegraph Companies
Telephone Companies
Television Sets & Parts
Tennis Supplies
Tents
Theme Parks
Thread
Tire Chains
Toasters
Tobacco
Tonics
Tools
Tourism
Tours
Toys
Track Lighting
Tractors, Farm
Travel Agencies
Trees & Tree Surgery
Trimmings
Trucks
Trunks
Trust Companies
Tubes, Inner
Tubes, Radio & Television
Twine
Typewriters

U

Umbrellas
Unions

V

Vacuum Cleaners
Vermouth
Vitamins

W

Wagons
Wallpaper

Y

Yachts
Yarns

1.6 Brands

Each of the 600 or so categories in the previous section have numerous brands that all compete for market share. This presents a tremendous opportunity for the savvy solicitor. With a complete sponsor analysis you will always outmaneuver the competition.

Brands Index

Air Fresher Solid
Renuzit
Stick Ups
Airwick
Glade

Airlines
Air New Zealand
America West
American
British Airways
Contenital
Delta
NorthWest
SouthWest
US Air

All Purpose Cleaners
409
Ajax
Fantastic
Lestoil
Mr. Clean
Pine-Sol
Spic-n-Span
Tackle
Top Job
X-14
Lime Away

Asprin
Advil
Anacin
Arthritis Foundation
Bayer
Bayer Childrens
Bufferin
Excedrin
Midol
Tylenol
Nuprin

Automotive
Audi
BMW
Buick
Cadillac
Dodge
Ford
Jaguar
Landrover
Mercedes
Rolls Royce
Saab
Yugo

Baby Care
Johnson's
Wet Ones
Huggies
Dryers

Bacon
Amour
Oscar Mayer
Hormel

Bank
Bank America
Chase Manhattan
First Interstate
First Union
Nations

Breakfast Bars
Nature Valley
Quaker
Kellogg's
Snack Wells
Nabisco

Breakfast Sausage
Jimmy Dean

Hormell
Bryan Cocktail

Brokerage Firms
Charles Schwab
Dean Witter
Legg Mason
Lehman Brothers
Kidder, Peabody & Co.
Merrill Lynch
PaineWebber
Prudential

Cereal
Almond Delight
Alpha Bits
Apple Jacks
Boobery
Bran Chex
Bran Flakes
Cap-n Crunch
Cheerios
Cinnamon Crunch
Corn Flakes
Corn Pops
Fiber One
Frosted Flakes
Grape Nuts
Kellogg's
Kix
Life
Lucky Charms
Malt-o-Meal
Nature Valley
Nutri Grain
Oatmeal Crisp
Puffed Wheat
Quaker Corn Bran
Raisin Nut Bran
Rice Chex
Special K

Brands Index

Cheese
Borden
County Line
Land O Lake's
Weight Watchers

Coffee Instant
Folgers
General Food Int'l
High Point
Maxwell House
Taster's

Credit Card
American Express
Discover
MasterCard
VISA

Deodorant
Arm & Hammer
Arid Solid
Ban Roll On
Ban Solid
Dial Solid
Dry Idea
Secret Roll On
Soft & Dry
Degree Roll On

Dish Detergent
Ajax
Dawn
Ivory
Joy
Palmolive
Sunlight

Document Processing
Canon
Konica
Xerox

Furniture Polish
Endust
Favor
Old English
Pledge

Greeting Card
American Greetings
Hallmark

Hotel
Four Seasons
Hilton
Holiday Inn
Hyatt
ITT Sheraton
Westin

Ice Cream
Bon Bons
Breyers
Drumstick Cones
Flintstone Pushup
Goldrush Bars
Good Humor
Klondike Bars
Polar Bars
Sealtest Ice Cream
Haagen Dazs
Blue Bell

Jams, Jellies & Perserves
Bama
Kraft
Smuckers
Welch's

Juices
Campbells Tomato
Chiquita
Dole Pineapple
Hawaiian Punch

Hi-C
Minute Maid
Mott's
Ocean Spray
Real Lemon
Sunny Delight
Tree-Top
V-8
Tropicana

Ketchup
Heinz
Hunt's

Kraft Cheese
American Singles
Cheddar
Cracker Barrell
Deluxe American Swiss
Grated Parmesan
Lite-n-lively
Philadelphia Cream
Philadelphia Soft
Velveeta
Whiz

Laundry Powder
All
Arm & Hammer
Biz
Bold
Cheer
Dash
Fab
Fresh Start
Gain
Oxydol
Surf
Tide
Ivory Snow

Brands Index

Laxatives & Stomach
Alka Seltzer
Citrucel
Correctol
Dairy Ease
Fibercon
Immodium
Maalox
Metamucil
Pepto Bismol
Preparation H

Lotion
Jergen's
Ken
Lubridem
Soft Sense
Vaseline Intensive Care

Macaroni
American Beauty
Creamette
Skinner

Mail Delivery
Airborne
United Parcel Service
United Postal Service

Margarine
Blue Bonnet
Fleisherman's
Imperial
Mazola
Parkey
Promise
Shedd's
Weight Watcher's

Orange Juice
Citris Hill
Donald Duck
Five Alive
Minute Maid
Sunkist
Tropicana

Peanut Butter
Jiff
Peter Pan
Reeses
Skippy
Smuckers

Potato Chips
Frito Lay
Pringles

Shampoo
Denorex
Finesse
Head-N-Shoulders
Ivory
Johnson's Baby
Loreal
Pantene
Pert Shampoo
Prell Liquid
Salon Selectives
Suave
Flex
Herbal Essence

Snacks
Chips Ahoy
Frito Lay
Slim Jim
Chex-Mix

Tea
Lipton's
Nestea

Toilet Bowl Cleaner
2000 Flushes
Bully
Liquid Plumer
Vanish

Trash Bags
Glad
Trail Kitchen

Vitamin
Centrum
Nature Made
One-A-Day
Ensure

Yogurt
Breyer's
Dannon
Light & Lively
Whitney's
Yoplait

1.7   Sponsorship Opportunities

Many properties are well-versed in dealing with corporate sponsors, staff members work hard and audiences can be targeted by specific demographic segment or as a whole to reach almost all demographic segments. Below is an extensive list of sponsorship opportunities that may be presented to sponsors:

SPONSORSHIP OPPORTUNITIES BY CATEGORY

Aerobics/Fitness
Air Shows
Amateur Sports Teams
Aquariums
Aquatics
Archery
Arts Festivals
Athletics
Auto Racing
  IndyCar
  Oval
  Rally
  Stock Cars
  Vintage
Ballooning
Baseball
Basketball
  3-on-3
Biathlons
Billiards
Bowling
Business Conferences
Business Lunches
Canoeing/Kayaking
Causes
  Arts
  Education
  Environment/Conservation
  Health
  Hunger
  Social
  Youth
Charity Benefits
Cheerleading
Children's Festival
City/Community Celebrations

Concerts
Cowboy Festivals
Cowboy Poetry Festivals
Cycling
  Mountain Bike
  Races
  Rides
Dance Companies
Dance Festivals
Drum Corps Competitions
Equine - Breed Registries
Equine Competitions
  Cutting Horses
  Dressage
  Grand Prixs
  Show Jumping
  Steeplechase/Hunting
Ethnic Festivals
  African American
  Cajun
  German
  Greek
  Hispanic
  Irish
  Italian
  Jewish
  Multicultural
  Native American
  Scandinavian
  Scottish
Expos
  African American
  Agricultural
  Antiques/Collectibles
  Arts
  Auto

Expos (cont.)
  Classic Automobiles
  Deaf
  Family
  Fashion
  Flower/Garden
  Generation X
  Golf
  Health/Fitness
  Hispanic
  Home
  Home/Garden
  Music
  Scientific
  Seniors
  Skiing/Snowboarding
  Sports/Outdoors
  Wedding
  Women
  Youth
Fencing
Figure Skating
Film Festivals
First Night Celebrations
Fishing
Folk Festivals
Football
Golf
Government
Gymnastics
Handball
Haunted Houses
Hockey
Holiday Festivals
Horse Racing
Ice Shows

Ice Skating
In-Line Skating
Interscholastic Sports
Jet Skiing
Kayaking
Kite Festivals
Lacrosse
Lifeguard Competitions
Membership Organizations
Military Recreation
Military Tattoos
Motorcycle Racing
Motorist Assistance
Museums
Music Festivals
   Bluegrass
   Blues
   Classical/Chamber/Opera
   Concert/Band
   Country
   Ethnic
   Folk
   Gospel
   Internet
   Jazz
   Oldies
   Reggae
   Rock/Pop
   World Music
National TV Programming
Off-the-Wall Events
Olympics
Opera Companies
Paddleball
Parades
Performing Arts Festivals
Performing Arts Presenters
Performing Arts Series

Photography Workshops
Players Assn. Marketing Arms
Polo
Powerboating
Pro Sports Teams
Promotion Councils
Radio Programs
Recreation & Park Districts
Renaissance Festivals
Rodeos
   Hispanic
Rowing
Rugby
Running/Walking
Sanctioning Bodies
Sports Leagues
Skiing
   Alpine
   Freestyle
   Nordic
   Snowboarding
   Water
Soccer
Softball
Sporting Clays
Sports & Social Clubs
Sports Entertainment
Sports Facilities
Sports Festivals
Squash
State Celebrations
State County Fairs
Storytelling Festivals
Symphonies/Orchestras
Syndicated TV Specials
Taste/Food Specials
Tenant Appreciation Parties
Tennis

Theater Companies
Theater Festivals
Touring Attractions
   Circuses
   Family Entertainment
   Firefighter Challenges
   IMAX Movies
   Performing Arts
   Virtual Reality
Triathlons
TV Broadcasts
Venues
   Amphitheaters
   Amusement Parks
   Arenas/Stadiums
   Auditoriums
   Fairgrounds
   Hotels/Casinos
   Ice Skating Rinks
   Malls/Developments
   Racetracks/Speedways
   Science Centers
   Sports Facilities
   Theme Parks
   Theme Restaurants
   University Recreation Ctr.
Volleyball
Walking/Striding
Windsurfing
World's Fairs
Yacht Racing
Zoos

The reality is that sponsorship opportunities exist around every corner. These examples are intended to stretch your imagination. You will be surprised how prevalent sponsorship is, once you begin to fully understand it. The next 6 pages provide examples of sponsorship in action.

1.8 Sponsorship Levels

There are numerous options for both recognizing and acknowledging your sponsors, many of which have not been conceived. In this business you can be as creative as you like as long as you are serving your needs, as well as, those of your sponsors. The higher the level, the higher the price and of course the more benefits.

Title Sponsor: The main or primary sponsor's name could either be incorporated into the sponsorship opportunity, or be attached to it.

      Examples:

                Reebok Challenge

                Mercedes Grand Slam

Presenting Sponsor: The presenting sponsor is recognized in many ways. Generally it is at a level below the title sponsor, unless there is no title sponsor. The presenting sponsors name could fall ahead of or after the sponsorship opportunity.

      Examples:
                Timberland
                presents
        The International Iron Man Contest

          Maine Flower/Garden Expo
                presented by
                Black & Decker

Co-Sponsor: Recognized with others of similar caliber. You may choose one title or presenting sponsor, and acknowledge all others as co-sponsors.

      Examples:
          AAU Junior Olympic Games
                co-sponsored by
                NIKE and Fox TV

                America's Cup
                co-sponsored by
            Rolex and Range Rover

1.9   Sponsor Benefits

Here is where you offer specific tangible and intangible assets to meet those motives we discussed in section 1.4. There are two primary sources of assets which properties can offer sponsors:

QUANTITATIVE ASSETS - tangible offerings

MEDIA
These assets help you build one customer at a time - the goal of every property. From television to live remotes, you'll be able to focus on your target market and garner more sponsorship revenue for every media dollar you spend.

- Advertorial
- Balloons
- Billboards
- Blimps
- Subway & Bus advertising
- Infomercials
- Television broadcasts
- Television commercials
- Promotional spots
- Remnant space
- Remotes

MINI-MEDIA
Mini-Media allows you to pay attention to the details and take advantage of every sponsor recognition opportunity. You'll immediately start thinking about the use of your brochures to generate additional sales, your stationary to position your sponsorship opportunity, and newsletters to induce sponsorship renewals.

- Brochures
- Banners
- Posters
- Newsletters
- Fliers
- Coupons
- Booklets
- Circulars
- Door hangers
- Gift certificates
- Stationary

TARGETED MEDIA

Sponsors get a higher rate of response by using your targeted media and in the long run generate a more loyal following, than their traditional marketing which generally tries to stuff their messages into as many mailboxes as possible.

- Customer Mailing lists
- Postcards
- Inserts
- Catalogs
- Database Marketing

PROMOTION

An effective promotion can put your sponsor's product or service in your audiences mind and keep it there. A contest, and unique promotional package will help you break through the clutter and reach your prospects directly.

- Lotteries
- Sweepstakes
- Contests
- Music
- Jingles
- Packaging
- Frequent buyer programs
- Point of purchase (POP)
- Point of sale (POS)
- Premiums
- Specialty Gifts
- Booths

NON-MEDIA

Often what sets successful products apart is the relationship that they build with their consumers. These assets provide sponsor's with a vehicle to earn their customer's trust, amaze them with service, and make them feel that they care about them in a way their competitors do not.

- Logo Usage
- Personal appearances
- Celebrities
- Endorsements
- Testimonials

- Market research
- News coverage
- Public service announcements
- Graphic design services
- Commercial printing
- Copywriting services
- Volunteers
- Advertisers
- Creative and video production
- Advertising sales support
- Internal publications
- Commercial spot production
- Voice overs
- Listener lines
- Multiple vendor resources
- Ticket and coupon outlets
- Imprinted grocery bags
- Imprinted stuffers
- Imprinted register receipts
- Banners
- Shelf talkers
- Bottle hangers

QUALITATIVE ASSETS - intangible offerings

- Awareness level of your sponsorship opportunity
- Prestige of program
- Desirability of the audience to the sponsor
- Length of "window of opportunity"
- Client entertainment opportunities
- Sponsorship execution expertise
- The loyalty of your audience
- Category exclusivity
- Hospitality opportunities with celebrities

1.10 Sponsorship Payment

This is where you ask for cash, products or services in exchange for the benefits you have provided the sponsor access to the benefits discussed in the previous section. Promotional consideration derived from sponsors is unrestricted. You can use it for the sponsorship opportunity being proposed or to relieve your general or departmental budgets.

Cash: promotional consideration paid in the form of cash.
Promotional Consideration: $30,000

Product: promotional consideration paid with products which are budget relieving. Also can be used to generate revenue during the event (i.e., T-shirts).
Promotional Consideration: $22,000 (new car)

Service: promotional consideration paid by providing a service which is budget relieving or can be used as additional assets in targeted sponsorship proposals (i.e., 30:sec Radio Spots)
Promotional Consideration: $15,000 (Airfare Credits)

Combination: promotional consideration paid by providing a combination of either cash, product or service.
Promotional Consideration: $80,000 ($65,000 Cash / $15,000 Airfare Credits)

The most comprehensive and affordable, step-b-step sponsorship recruitment training program on the market!

Sponsorship Recruitment 101-102™
Self-Study Course

Module Two

SPONSORSHIP ACQUISTION

Systematic Approach To Obtaining Sponsorship

Anthony B. Miles
With Renee Crenshaw

2.0   Sponsorship Acquisition

The underlying principle to my *Systems Approach to Sponsorship Acquisition™* is to develop and implement cost-effective solutions and create engaging and instructionally sound sponsorship acquisition professionals. A systems approach is used to ensure that optimum performance is achieved.

This course is based on my Seminar entitled *How To Produce Millions In Corporate Sponsorship*. This manual provides acquisition professionals with the background information they must know if they plan to start or improve an existing program. Our seminar is designed to provide students with practical insights into the world of sponsorship.

This course is taught at an introductory and advanced level.

The *introductory level* exposes solicitors to general sponsorship theory and the application of this theory to property structure and design.

At the *advanced level* you're asked to write an extensive property plan for a sponsorship opportunity you ultimately will market.

The Systems Approach To Sponsorship Acquisition™

The International Money Group model is a eight phase process that is used to secure sponsors. The eight phases are shown below. Phases 4-8 form a continuous loop.

Phase 1.	**Prepare** your property for sponsorship	**(Module 3)**
Phase 2.	**Perform** an internal analysis	**(Module 4)**
Phase 3.	**Design** a property plan	**(Module 5)**
Phase 4.	**Conduct** a Sponsor Analysis	**(Module 6)**
Phase 5.	**Create** Sponsorship Packages	**(Module 7)**
Phase 6.	**Recruit** Sponsors	**(Module 8)**
Phase 7.	**Develop** a Customized Proposal	**(Module 9)**
Phase 8.	**Execute** Sponsorship	**(Module 10)**

Phase 1.   ***Prepare*** your property for sponsorship   ***(Module 3)***

The structure of properties*.* Properties are complex collages consisting of people, processes and technology. Put together properly you have a well-oiled machine. In this module you are exposed to these infrastructures so you understand how to put yours together. Here are the **6** steps to success:

1. ***Review*** the characteristics, knowledge, skill and ability of million dollar sponsorship producers
2. ***Set-up*** your properties organizational structure
3. ***Select*** your acquisition team
4. ***Document*** policies and procedures
5. ***Train*** members of your staff, Board of Directors and volunteers
6. ***Set*** your budget

Phase 2.   ***Perform*** an internal analysis   ***(Module 4)***

Property assets and markets. The challenge facing a property manager is deciding how to devise innovative benefits and market expansion strategies so their property can gain a presence. This requires that they understand quite a bit about their salable assets and demographics. Here is your **3** steps to success:

1. ***Define*** properties mission
2. ***Identify*** your properties audience
3. ***Assess*** your property

Phase 3.   *Design* property plan   *(Module 5)*

Putting your property plan together. Phase three is the design of the properties objectives, methodologies, structure and plan of action. The property plan makes extensive use of the information in Phases one and two. Here are the *10* steps to success:

1. ***Fabricate*** *cover page*
2. ***Work-up*** *your table of contents*
3. ***Create*** *your executive summary*
4. ***State*** your business/industry description
5. ***Describe*** your sponsorship opportunity
6. ***Outline*** organizational data
7. ***Devise*** market strategy
8. ***Perform*** competitive analysis
9. ***Describe*** your operations plan
10. ***Prepare*** budget information

Phase 4.   *Conduct* Sponsor Analysis   *(Module 6)*

Conducting Sponsor Analysis. The goal of Phase four is to foster an appreciation of sponsor analysis, and help the solicitor become a wise user of it. With an informed practical approach sponsorship acquisition professional can better decide which corporations would benefit from their sponsorship opportunity. Here are the *8* steps to success:

1. ***Define*** your target sponsors by category
2. ***Describe*** sponsor categories active role
3. ***Choose*** 6 brands in each category
4. ***Identify*** the decision maker and evaluation criteria
5. ***Zero-in*** on the sponsor's decision making deadlines and budget periods
6. ***Reveal*** clients and suppliers
7. ***Analyze*** current and past sponsorships
8. ***Uncover*** *their salable assets*

Phase 5.   ***Create*** Sponsorship Packages   ***(Module 7)***

Sponsorship Packages. The fifth phase involves setting your sponsorship opportunity structure and determining which sponsor's get what benefits. The end result are standard packages which will be customized in Phase seven based on the information gathered in phase six. Here are the **4** steps to success:

1. ***Establish*** sponsorship levels
2. ***Survey*** your assets
3. ***Determine*** distribution of benefits
4. ***Come*** to terms with media

Phase 6.   *Recruit* Sponsors   *(Module 8)*

Recruiting Sponsors. It wasn't long ago when acts associated with sponsoring properties were fairly rudimentary. Today it involves a sophisticated analysis of targeted sponsors, property communication needs and what competitors are offering. Only then can a solicitor demonstrate why his sponsorship opportunity is potentially more effective than other opportunities a company could sponsor. Here are the *4* steps to success:

1. *Gather* target lists
2. *Design* marketing communications
3. *Interview* sponsors
4. *Analyze* data

Phase 7.   *Develop* Customized Proposal   *(Module 9)*

Construction of proposals. The seventh phase is the development of customized persuasive proposals. The sponsor analysis and sponsorship recruitment phases is used to direct the development of the proposal and their enabling objectives. Here are the *11* steps to success:

1. *Acquire* the winning attitude
2. *Analyze* sponsor analysis
3. *Develop* proposal schedule
4. *Establish* marketing strategy
5. *Create* outline, executive summaries and story boards
6. *Draft* proposal content
7. *Determine* proposal pricing
8. *Evaluate* proposal
9. *Package* & deliver proposal
10. *Make* presentation
11. *Monitor* Decision Process

Phase 8. *Execute* Sponsorship   *(Module 10)*

Sponsorship In Action. Once you have been successful in obtaining sponsorship for your property, it is essential that your property follow through on all the promises undertaken, to give your property every chance of obtaining the sponsor's support in the future. Here are the *3* steps to success:

1. *Draft* agreement
2. *Plan* the sponsorship opportunity
3. *Establish* continuous communication with sponsor

The most comprehensive and affordable, step-b-step sponsorship recruitment training program on the market!

Sponsorship Recruitment 101-102™
Self-Study Course

Module Three

SPONSORSHIP PREPARATION

Internal Readiness

Anthony B. Miles
With Renee Crenshaw

3.0   Sponsorship Preparation

I believe that millions in cash, products and services can be produced every year and dramatic increases in production can be realized by *analyzing your property*, *your marketplace* and *internal readiness* before beginning. In this module we start with internal readiness and cover analyzing your property, and your marketplace in the next module.

"It takes organization, dedication and persistence to create a successful sponsorship program"

Internal readiness is essential to the success of your overall sponsorship acquisition efforts. The goal of assessing organizational readiness is to determine the areas of the property that needs to be strengthened prior to expanding or starting a new sponsorship program. It is important to prioritize those areas and to prepare a plan that will improve those areas in a timely manner. Developing and refining key systems is the most effective way to increase the operating capacity of any property.

Test your readiness by taking a few moments to answer the following questions:

Sponsorship Acquisition Readiness Test

Does Your Property Have These Items In Place

A set organizational structure
Yes___   No___

A sponsorship acquisition team
Yes___   No___

Duties and responsibilities for team members
Yes___   No___

A set sponsorship acquisition budget
Yes___   No___

Sponsor customer service representatives
Yes___   No___

A sponsorship filing system
Yes___   No___

Tax saving bookkeeping system
Yes___   No___

On-going sponsorship training program for staff, Board members and volunteers
Yes___   No___

Sponsorship policies and procedures approved by board
Yes___   No___

Acquisition Timeline
Yes___   No___

If the answer is "no" to any of these questions, you are not prepared to continue sponsorship acquisition.

Sponsorship recruitment can be a complex, confusing and painstaking process. It takes organization, dedication and persistence to create a successful sponsorship program. If you are an organized, detailed oriented person who can follow these 9 steps, your odds for obtaining sponsorship will increase.

1. **Review** the characteristics, knowledge, skill and ability of million dollar sponsorship producers
2. **Set-up** your properties organizational structure
3. **Determine** acquisition team roles
4. **Select** your acquisition team
5. **Document** policies and procedures
6. **Train** members of your staff, Board of Directors and volunteers
7. **Set** your budget
8. **Set-up** tax-saving bookkeeping system
9. **Develop** acquisition schedule

Step 1. **Review** the Characteristics, Knowledge, Skills and Abilities of Million Dollar Sponsorship Producers

My studies have show that the personalities and individual characteristics of million dollar sponsorship producers may be the most important factor for success.

An individual's management skills have become so important that sponsor's have begun to revise the way they look at potential sponsorship deals. Rather than betting on the "horse" (i.e., the sponsorship opportunity), they are more likely to bet on the "jockey" and look at someone who has a history of successful past sponsorship efforts. Sponsors have come to realize a good sponsorship opportunity that reaches their demographics does not necessarily guarantee their return on investment, but a good sponsorship acquisition professional can, determine whether the sponsorship opportunity is optimal or not.

Your personal development is extremely important. Compare your characteristics and the skills, knowledge and abilities described on the next two pages and see how many you possess. Obviously, no one will display all the qualities, but this review will help you assess your potential to become a million dollar producer.

11 Characteristics of million dollar sponsorship producers
Check off the degree to which each characteristic on the list describes you.
V= Very much like me, S = Somewhat like me, N = Not like me at all.

Million dollar sponsorship producers typically:

1. Are decisive decision makers.   **V S N**
Million dollar sponsorship producers tend to make decisions early and instinctively and are often forced to rely on their judgement and make decisions without complete information. If you agonize over decisions this is not you.

2. Enjoy taking charge.   **V S N**
Million dollar sponsorship producers enjoy taking charge and following through to the end. They are good at finishing projects, getting closure as well as grabbing projects from the start.

3. Want to be the master of their funding destiny.   **V S N**
Million dollar sponsorship producers typically have less desire to get rich as "to meet the needs of their property" and prove that their sponsorship opportunity is superior to the competition. In fact these individuals make less money than they would working for themselves. Their real income is psychic income, the satisfaction that comes out of meeting the needs of their sponsors.

4. Are organized, independent and self-confident.   **V S N**
Million dollar sponsorship producers have few people to rely on. They must be able to perform all the phases of sponsorship acquisition alone.

5. Are hard workers.   **V S N**
Million dollar sponsorship producers usually work longer, harder and more stressful hours, largely because they have no one to rely on.

6. Come from a fundraising background.   **V S N**
Sponsorship acquisition professionals who have been involved in fundraising have a better chance of success. They are generally able to understand the sacrifices required by Million dollar sponsorship producers, and know what they are getting into from the start.

7. Can take criticism.   **V S N**
Million dollar sponsorship producer must be able to take criticism and rejection and bounce back with a positive aspect. If you turn off at the first sign of trouble, you are probably not the right kind of person who will produce millions.

8. Have specialized marketing ability from experience or education. **VSN**
Sponsorship is heavy on marketing. Individuals who enter an area which they are familiar, either by education or experience, have a higher probability of success.

9. Are determined and persistent. **V S N**
Million dollar sponsorship producers tend to go where angels fear to tread. They must be able to successfully avoid nagging doubts and "keep on keepin' on."

10. Can find people to compensate for weaknesses, are good judges of talent and character. **V S N**
Typically, a million dollar sponsorship producer's major problem is people. It is necessary to assemble a team to make up the knowledge, skill and ability they lack.

11. Can see how all parts fit together. **V S N**
As the leader of the charge you have to wear many hats: Marketing, accounting, legal, bookkeeping, sponsor recruitment, sponsor relations and more. It is necessary to see how these different pieces fit together to form the entirety of the property.

Think about your responses to the questions. If you circled "very much like me" for the majority, you probably have what it takes to become the next million dollar producer. If you circled "not like me at all" for the majority of these qualities, you may lack the characteristics needed to succeed in sponsorship acquisition.

Your characteristics are only one part of the million dollar sponsorship producer feasibility analysis. Your next step is to determine whether or not you possess the knowledge, skill or ability.

Required knowledge, skills and abilities

KNOWLEDGE OF:
- practices and methods used in sponsorship acquisition.
- tax laws.
- intellectual properties.

SKILLS:
- negotiations.
- team building.

ABLITY TO:
- balance marketing/cost/schedule requirements.
- evaluate problems, and implement solutions.
- communicate effectively.
- calculate Return On Investment (ROI).
- keep track of sponsor recruitment and make reports.
- prepare simple agreements, marketing communications and customized proposals.

Step 2. *Set-up* your properties organizational structure

A key element in successfully developing and implementing any sponsorship program is establishing clear, roles and responsibilities for various individuals and groups that will be working on it. However, the composition, roles and responsibilities of any sponsorship program may vary depending on the complexity, size and duration of the sponsorship opportunity.

Adopt an appropriate organizational structure to suit your particular sponsorship program. The organization structure used within most properties is shown in figure 3-1.

PROPERTY ORGANIZATION

Figure 3-1. Sponsorship organization chart.

As you can see, the sponsorship acquisition manager acts as the central communication interface with all parties involved in the sponsorship program.

The *Sponsorship Acquisition Manager* is the individual who has the ultimate responsibility and accountability for the program's success or failure. This individual intimately manages the program's activities. Specific responsibilities include:

• Assess/manage risk (and reports to upper management or executive committee as appropriate).
• Sets and communicates timelines.
• Manages budget.

- Manage acquisition team development and conflicts.
- Is key sponsor interface (with Sponsor Service Manager).
- Leads, directs, coaches, and supports the Acquisition Team.
- Prepares marketing communication and customized proposals.

"A Sponsorship Acquisition Manager wears many hats."

The **Acquisition Team** consists of a Sponsorship Acquisition Manager, Trainer, Marketing Director, Market Research Analyst, Graphic Designer, Auditor, Executive Committee, Public Relations and Communications Manager, Sponsor Service Manager and Advertising Manager. Typically acquisition team members will have responsibility for certain key tasks and:

- May manage activities with the program (specific to either what they have been assigned or their expertise).
- May be responsible for schedule and/or budget within the area of the program they manage.

**"The Acquisition Team should consist of the people most capable
of helping you secure the sponsorship."**

The **Sponsor** also plays a key role in any sponsorship. In addition to specific support included in the proposal. Other areas of responsibility include, but are not limited to:

- Providing a point of contact.
- Approving changes.
- Providing resources as required.
- Providing specifications.
- Attending progress review meetings.
- Participating in sponsorship evaluation.

Step 3. *Determine* acquisition team roles

Tools which can be used to define specific roles and results of members of the acquisition team with respect to the phases identified in module 2 is called the **Role Sheets**. These can be used for building the responsibility structure and team commitment to the program. The Role Sheets describe the roles and the results that need to be accomplished. The property organization structure identifies the people who need to be involved. The Role Sheet ties work to people by providing an easy format for identifying the individual's or organization's level of involvement in each acquisition activity. On the next 20 or so pages we have analyzed the roles of these major positions:

Sponsorship Acquisition Manager
Sponsorship Trainer
Sponsorship Acquisition Professional
Sponsorship Service Manager
Marketing Director
Graphic Designer
Auditor
Executive Committee
Public Relations and Communications Manager
Sponsor Service Manager
Advertising Manager

Position Title: Sponsorship Acquisition Manager

ROLE: **DEVELOPS SPONSORSHIP PROGRAM**
by:
identifying sponsorship opportunities; timelines; pricing,
integrated plans for sponsorship opportunity; developing
marketing strategies.

ESSENTIAL TASKS:

1.   **DETERMINE SPONSOR NEEDS AND DESIRES AND SPONSORSHIP OPPORTUNITY PRICING**
by:
specifying the research needed to obtain market information.

2.   **RECOMMENDS THE NATURE AND SCOPE OF PRESENT AND FUTURE SPONSORSHIP OPPORTUNITIES**
by:
appraising new sponsorship ideas and/or packaging changes.

3.   **ASSESSES MARKET COMPETITON**
by:
comparing the properties sponsorship opportunity to competitors.

4.   **PROVIDES SOURCE DATA FOR SPONSORSHIP OPPORTUNTIY COMMUNICATIONS**
by:
defining sponsorship opportunity marketing communication objectives.

5.   **OBTAINS SPONSORSHIP MARKET SHARE**
by:
working with the Sponsorship Acquisition Professional to develop sponsor
recruitment strategies.

6.   **ASSESSES SPONSOR ANALYSIS DATA**
by:
calling on potential sponsors and evaluating marketing communications results.

7. **PROVIDES INFORMATION TO MANAGEMENT**
   by:
   preparing short-term and long-term sponsorship sales forecasts and analysis; answering questions and requests.

8. **BRINGS NEW SPONSORSHIP OPPORTUNITIES TO MARKET**
   by:
   analyzing proposed sponsorship opportunity programs; preparing return-on-investment analyses; establishing time schedules with operations and marketing.

9. **INTRODUCES AND MARKETS NEW SPONSORSHIP OPPORTUNITIES**
   by:
   developing time integrated plans with sales, advertising, and production.

10. **DETERMINES SPONSORSHIP PACKAGE PRICING**
    by:
    utilizing industry pricing standards.

11. **COMPLETES OPERATIONAL REQUIREMENTS**
    by:
    scheduling and assigning employees; following up work results.

12. **MAINTAINS ACQUISITION TEAM**
    by:
    recruiting, selecting, orienting, and training team members.

Position Title: Sponsorship Trainer

ROLE: PREPARES ACQUISITION MANAGER AND TEAM MEMBERS
                              TO ACCOMPLISH ACQUISITION RESULTS
                              by:
                              presenting sponsorship training and development programs.

ESSENTIAL TASKS:

1.   SATISFIES TRAINING AND DEVELOPMENT NEEDS
         by:
         researching, designing, or learning sponsorship training programs.

2.   PRESENTS TRAINING AND DEVELOPMENT PROGRAMS
         by:
         identifying sponsorship learning objectives; selecting instructional
         methodologies.

3.   REINFORCES LEARNING
         by:
         selecting and utilizing sponsorship training media.

4.   EVALUATES TRAINING AND DEVELOPMENT EFFECTIVENESS
         by:
         assessing application of learning to job performance; recommending future
         training and development programs.

5.   PREPARES TRAINING AND RESOURCE MANUALS
         by:
         identifying purpose; assembling and composing information.

6.   MAINTAIN KNOWLEDGE OF SPONSORSHIP METHODOLOGIES
         by:
         attending workshops; reviewing professional publications; establishing personal
         networks; participating in professional societies.

7.   CONTRIBUTES TO TEAM EFFORT
         by:
         accomplishing related results as needed.

Position Title:	Sponsorship Acquisition Professional

ROLE: **OBTAINS SPONSORSHIP**
by:
promoting the sponsorship opportunity benefits to sponsors.

ESSENTIAL TASKS:

1. **ESTABLISHES SPONSORSHIP ACQUSITION GOALS**
    by:
    studying properties objectives and needs; advising board of directors (if applicable).

2. **GUIDES SPONSORSHIP ACQUISITION EFFORTS**
    by:
    formulating sponsorship acquisition policies, procedures, and programs, including arrangement for the delivery of product or service sponsorship, obtaining sponsorship consultants.

3. **IDENTIFY POTENTIAL SPONSORS**
    by:
    analyzing budgets; examining demographics and establishing personal networks.

4. **PREPARES PROMOTIONAL LITERATURE AND PRESENTATIONS**
    by:
    composing copy; designing layout; obtaining graphic arts advice; and contracting with printers.

5. **RECRUITS SPONSORS**
    by:
    mailing literature; answering inquires; preparing proposals; assigning solicitation to board members, volunteers, and staff members; making personal visits, speeches, and promotions.

6. **ORGANIZES PROMOTIONS**
    by:
    setting objectives; targeting demographics; developing approaches; making solicitations.

7. **ORGANIZES SPECIAL EVENTS**
    by:
    identifying special guests; developing announcements and invitations; making and coordinating arrangements; supervising activities.

8. **OBTAINS HELP TO ACCOMPLISH OBJECTIVES**
   by:
   recruiting, scheduling, training and supervising volunteers.

9. **PREPARES SPONSORSHIP ACQUISITION REPORTS**
   by:
   collecting, analyzing, and summarizing information.

10. **CONTRIBUTES TO TEAM EFFORT**
    by:
    accomplishing related results as needed.

Position Title: **Sponsorship Service Manager**

POSITION PURPOSE: **MAINTAINS SPONSOR SATISFACTION**
by:
defining and developing product, service, and problem solving information; training and maintaining staff to provide information and resolve problems.

ESSENTIAL TASKS:

1. **MEASURES SPONSOR PERCEPTIONS AND AWARENESS LEVELS OF SPONSORSHIP OPPORTUNITY**
   by:
   designing and implementing communication methodologies; validating results; tracking effectiveness of sponsorship.

2. **RESOLVES SPONSOR DISSATIFACTION**
   by:
   planning and directing the receipt, investigation, evaluation, and setting of complaints and claims; following up with sponsors; personally resolving difficult situations.

3. **RESOLVES DISCREPENCIES**
   by:
   consulting with other acquisition team members; collecting and analyzing information.

4. **AUTHORIZES RETENTION OF DATA**
   by:
   analyzing future applicability of complaint resolution information.

5. **MAINTAINS SPONSOR SERVICE OPERATIONS**
   by:
   initiating, coordinating, and enforcing program, operational, policies and procedures.

Position Title: Public Relations and Communications Manager

ROLE: **MAINTAINS PUBLIC AWARENESS OF PROPERTY ISSUES**
by:
planning and directing external and internal information programs.

ESSENTIAL TASKS:

1.   **SUPPORTS PROPERTY GOALS AND OBJECTIVES**
by:
developing external and internal information programs.

2.   **IDENTIFIES EXTERNAL AND INTERNAL INFORMATION NEEDS**
by:
researching trends; conducting surveys and analyzing responses; information requests.

3.   **PLANS EXTERNAL AND INTERNAL INFORMATION PROGRAMS**
by:
identifying audiences and information needs; determining specific media approaches.

4.   **INFORMS PUBLIC AND STAFF**
by:
developing and disseminating information, including fact sheets, news releases, newsletters, photographs, films, recordings, personal appearances, etc.; purchasing advertising space and time.

5.   **RESPONDS TO MEDIA**
by:
recommending information strategies to management; planning responses; providing information; arranging interviews and tours; editing copy; coaching responders.

6.   **MAINTAINS RAPPORT WITH MEDIA REPRESENTATIVES**
by:
arranging continuing contacts; resolving concerns.

7. **PROVIDES OPINION, OFFERS SUPPORT, AND GATHERS INFORMATION**
   by:
   representing the organization at public, social, and business events.

8. **ACCOMPLISHES SPECIFIC INFORMATION OBJECTIVES**
   by:
   designing and conducting special projects; establishing relationships with consultants and others.

9. **MAINTAIN HISTORICAL REFERENCE**
   by:
   establishing and maintaining a filing and retrieval system.

10. **ACHIEVES FINANCIAL OBJECTIVES**
    by:
    preparing an annual budget; scheduling expenditures; analyzing variances; initiating corrective action.

11. **COMPLETES PUBLIC RELATIONS AND COMMUNICATIONS OPERATIONAL REQUIREMENTS**
    by:
    scheduling and assigning employees; following up on the results.

12. **MAINTAINS PUBLIC RELATIONS AND COMMUNICATIONS STAFF**
    by:
    recruiting, selecting, orienting, and training staff.

Position Title: **Marketing Director**

ROLE: **DEVELOPS MARKETING STRATEGY**
by:
studying advertising promotions; tracking new product launches; identifying sponsors and their current and future needs; monitoring the competition.

ESSENTIAL TASKS:

1. **CONTRIBUTES TO MARKETING EFFECTIVENESS**
    by:
    identifying short-term and long-range issues that must be addressed; recommending options and courses of action; implementing directives.

2. **OBTAINS MARKET SHARE**
    by
    developing marketing plans and programs for each sponsorship opportunity; directing promotional support.

3. **MAINTAINS RELATIONS WITH SPONSORS**
    by:
    organizing and developing specific sponsor relations programs; determining company presence at conferences, chamber meetings, seminars and trade shows.

4. **PROVIDES SHORT- AND LONG-TERM MARKET FORECASTS AND REPORTS**
    by:
    directing market research collection, analysis, and implementation of market data.

5. **INFLUENCES PRESENT AND FUTURE SPONSORSHIP OPPORTUNITY**
    by:
    determining and evaluating current and future sponsor marketing trends.

6.   **DEVELOPS NEW USES FOR EXISTING SPONSORSHIP OPPORTUNITIES**
     by:
     analyzing statistics regarding sponsor development; acquiring and analyzing data; consulting with internal and external sources.

7.   **MAINTAINS SPONSOR DATA BASE**
     by:
     identifying and assembling marketing information.

8.   **ACHIEVE FINANCIAL OBJECTIVES**
     by:
     preparing an annual budget; scheduling expenditures; analyzing variances; initiating corrective actions.

Position Title: Accountant

ROLE: **PROVIDES FINANCIAL INFORMATION TO TEAM**
by:
researching and analyzing accounting data; preparing
reports.

ESSENTIAL TASKS:

1.   **PREPARES ASSET, LIABILITY, AND CAPITAL ACCOUNT ENTRIES**
by:
compiling and analyzing account information.

2.   **DOCUMENTS FINANCIAL TRANSACTIONS**
by:
entering account information.

3.   **RECOMMENDS FINANCIAL ACTIONS**
by:
analyzing accounting options.

4.   **SUMMARIES CURRENT FINANCIAL STATUS**
by:
collecting information; preparing balance sheet, profit and loss statement, and
other reports.

5.   **SUBSTATIATES FINANCIAL TRANSACTIONS**
by:
auditing documents.

6.   **MAINTAINS ACCOUNTING CONTROLS**
by:
preparing and recommending policies and procedures.

7. **RECONCILES FINANCIAL DISCREPANIES**
   by:
   collecting and analyzing account information.

8. **SECURES FINANCIAL INFORMATION**
   by:
   completing data base backups.

9. **MAINTAINS FINANCIAL SECURITY**
   by:
   following internal controls.

10. **PREPARES PAYMENTS**
    by:
    verifying documentation, and requesting disbursements.

Position Title: Risk and Insurance Manager

ROLE: CONTROL RISK AND LOSSES
by:
planning, directing, and coordinating risk and insurance programs.

ESSENTIAL TASKS:

1. **DETERMINE FINANCIAL IMPACT OF RISK ON PROPERTY**
    by:
    analyzing and classifying risk frequency and potential severity.

2. **MINIMIZES LOSSES**
    by:
    researching trends; conducting surveys and analyzing responses; and information requests.

3. **PLACES INSURANCE**
    by:
    directing insurance negotiations; selecting insurance brokers and carriers.

4. **COMPLIES WITH FEDERAL, STATE AND LOCAL LEGAL REQUIREMENTS**
    by:
    studying existing and new fidelity, surety, liability, property, group life, medical; anticipating changes.

5. **ALLOCATES PROGRAM COSTS**
    by:
    preparing operational and risk reports for analyses.

6. **DIRECTS LOSS PREVENTION AND SAFETY PROGRAMS**
    by:
    selecting and directing safety activities, and loss prevention experts.

7. **COMPLETES RISK MANAGEMENT OPERATIONAL REQUIREMENTS**
    by:
    scheduling and assigning employees; following up on work results.

Position Title: Accounts Receivable/Payable Clerk

ROLE: OBTAINS SPONSORSHIP REVENUE AND INVOICES
by:
verifying and completing payable and receivable transactions.

ESSENTIAL TASKS:

1.   **PREPARES WORK TO BE ACCOMPLISHED**
by:
preparing and sorting documents and related information.

2.   **PAYS INVOICES**
by:
verifying transaction information; scheduling and preparing disbursements; obtaining authorization of payment.

3.   **OBTAINS SPONSORSHIP REVENUE**
by:
verifying sponsorship payment information in agreement; preparing and mailing invoices.

5.   **PREPARES FINANCIAL REPORTS**
by:
recommending information strategies to management; planning responses; providing information; arranging interviews and tours; editing copy; coaching responders.

6.   **MAINTAINS ACCOUNTING LEDGERS**
by:
posting cash, products and service transactions.

7. **VERIFIES ACCOUNTS**
    by:
    reconciling statements and transactions.

9. **SECURES SPONSORSHIP INFORMATION**
    by:
    completing data base backups.

10. **MAINTAINS SPONSORSHIP HISTORICAL DATA**
    by:
    filing accounting documents.

11. **CONTRIBUTIONS TO TEAM EFFORTS**
    by:
    accomplishing related results as needed.

Position Title: **Sponsorship Development Consultant**

ROLE: **IMPROVES ORGANIZATIONAL RESULTS**
by:
assessing performance; diagnosing problems;
recommending courses of action.

ESSENTIAL TASKS:

1. **ASSESSES EFFECTIVENESS OF ORGANIZATION STRUCTURE**
   by:
   studying clarity of mission, strategy, objectives, priorities, accountabilities, and communication systems.

2. **ASSESSES UTILIZATION OF HUMAN RESOURCES**
   by:
   studying staffing resources, position results outcomes, succession plans, and sponsorship development.

3. **DIAGNOSE ORGANIZATION PROBLEMS**
   by:
   examining performance; surveying and interviewing managers and team members regarding efficiency, effectiveness, morale, climate, and profitability.

4. **RESOLVES ORGANIZATION PROBLEMS**
   by:
   presenting and evaluating options; guiding decisions; recommending courses of action.

5. **IMPROVES ORGANIZATION RESULTS**
   by:
   identifying potential sponsors; introducing new practices; presenting plan of action; defining and recommending policies and procedures; designing and conducting team building and sponsorship improvement training.

6. **MAINTAINS PROFESSIONAL AND TECHNICAL KNOWLEDGE**
   by:
   attending workshops; reviewing professional publications; establishing personal networks; participating in professional societies.

Position Title: Graphic Designer

ROLE: **PREPARE VISUAL PRESENTATIONS**
by:
designing art and copy layouts.

ESSENTIAL TASKS:

1.   **PREPARES WORK TO BE ACCOMPLISHED**
by:
gathering information and materials.

2.   **PLANS CONCEPT**
by:
studying information and materials.

3.   **ILLUSTRATES CONCEPT**
by:
designing rough layout of art and copy regarding arrangement, size, type size
and style, and related aesthetic concepts.

4.   **OBTAINS APPROVAL FOR CONCEPTS**
by:
submitting rough layout for approval.

5.   **PREPARES FINISHED COPY OF ART**
by:
operating typesetting, printing, and similar equipment; purchasing from vendors.

6.   **PREPARES FINAL LAYOUT**
by:
marking and pasting up finished copy and art.

7. **ENSURES OPERATION OF EQUIPMENT**
   by:
   completing preventative maintenance requirements; following manufacturer's instructions; troubleshooting malfunctions; calling for repairs, maintaining equipment inventories; evaluating new equipment.

8. **COMPLETES PROJECTS**
   by:
   designing and conducting special projects; establishing relationships with consultants and others.

9. **MAINTAIN TECHNICAL KNOWLEDGE**
   by:
   attending design workshops; reviewing professional publications; participating in professional societies.

10. **CONTRIBUTES TO TEAM EFFORT**
    by:
    accomplishing related results as needed.

Position Title: Sponsorship Executive Committee (Board member)

ROLE:
MEETS PROPERTY NEEDS
by:
determining and pursuing property goals; guiding property operations.

ESSENTIAL TASKS:

1. **ESTABLISHES AND MAINTAINS THE MISSION OF THE PROPERTY**
   by:
   identifying the properties demographic and sponsor needs; advocating property's beliefs.

2. **DETERMINES LONG-TERM GOALS OF THE PROPERTY**
   by:
   assessing sponsors needs; examining properties resources and capabilities; preparing a strategic plan.

3. **MANAGES PROPERTY OPERATIONS**
   by:
   employing, supporting, and advising the Chief Operations Officer.

4. **GUIDES PROPERTY OPERATIONS**
   by:
   approving operating structure, policy and procedure.

5. **MAINTAINS THE PROPERTIES SPONSORSHIP STABILITY**
   by:
   identifying requirements; soliciting sponsors; setting sponsorship budget; auditing procedures and practices.

6. **ASSURES ACHIEVEMENT OF PROPERTIES MISSION AND POLICIES**
   by:
   reviewing properties performance.

7. **MAINTAINS PROPERTIES EXECUTIVE COMMITTEE OPERATIONS**
   by:
   recruiting and electing executive committee members; establishing committee operating structure and policies.

8. **CONTRIBUTES TO TEAM EFFORT**
   by:
   accomplishing related results as needed.

9. **MAINTAIN HISTORICAL REFERENCE**
   by:
   establishing and maintaining a filing and retrieval system.

10. **ACHIEVES FINANCIAL OBJECTIVES**
    by:
    preparing an annual budget; scheduling expenditures; analyzing variances; initiating corrective action.

Position Title: Sponsorship Auditor

ROLE: **PROTECTS PROPERTY ASSETS**
by:
ensuring compliance with internal control procedures, and regulations.

ESSENTIAL TASKS:

1.   **ENSURES COMPLIANCE WITH ESTABLISHED INTERNAL CONTROL PROCEDURES**
by:
examining records, reports, operating practices, and documentation.

2.   **VERIFIES ASSETS**
by:
comparing items to documentation.

3.   **COMPLETES AUDIT REPORTS**
by:
documenting audit findings.

4.   **MAINTAINS INTERNAL CONTROL SYSTEMS**
by:
updating audit programs and questionnaires; recommending new policies and procedures.

5.   **COMMUNICATES AUDIT FINDINGS**
by:
preparing a final report; discussing findings with team members.

6.   **ASSURES ACHIEVEMENT OF PROPERTIES MISSION AND POLICIES**
by:
reviewing properties performance.

7.   **MAINTAIN TECHNICAL KNOWLEDGE**
by:
attending workshops; reviewing professional publications; participating in professional societies.

8.   **CONTRIBUTES TO TEAM EFFORT**
by:
accomplishing related results as needed.

Position Title: **Advertising Manager**

POSITION PURPOSE: **PROMOTES SPONSORSHIP OPPORTUNIITY**
by:
defining, developing, and implementing media and sales promotion programs.

ESSENTIAL TASKS:

1. **DEFINES ADVERTISING OBJECTIVES, CAMPAIGNS AND BUDGETS**
   by:
   studying marketing plans and consulting with property managers.

2. **SELECTS INTERNAL AND EXTERNAL VENDORS**
   by:
   determining production requirements.

3. **ACHIEVES ADVERTISING FINANCIAL OBJECTIVES**
   by:
   preparing an annual budget; scheduling expenditures; using combinations of internal/external resources; analyzing variances; initiating corrective actions.

4. **ENSURES SUPPLY OF PROMOTIONAL LITERATURE**
   by:
   monitoring inventories; keeping sponsorship opportunity information current.

5. **DEVELOPS ADVERTISING AND SALES PROMOTION PROGRAMS**
   by:
   utilizing media advertising, direct mail, trade shows, publicity, point-of-purchase, and audiovisual presentations.

6. **COMPLETES OPERATIONAL REQUIREMENTS**
   by:
   scheduling and assigning employees; following up on work results.

7. **MAINTAINS ADVERTISING STAFF**
   by:
   recruiting, selecting, orienting, and training employees.

8.   **MAINTAIN TECHNICAL KNOWLEDGE**
     by:
     attending design workshops; reviewing professional publications; participating in professional societies.

9.   **CONTRIBUTES TO TEAM EFFORT**
     by:
     accomplishing related results as needed.

Step 4. *Select* your acquisition team

Selecting a acquisition team is typically a formal process initiated after the decision is reached to start a program. Often the individual(s) who took the lead in getting the decision may accept responsibility for establishing a acquisition team and getting the program started. This process consists of sending copies of the roles to all parties and meeting to assign a Sponsorship Acquisition Manager and other members of the acquisition team.

The acquisition team should consist of the people with the combination of technical expertise and proposal writing experience needed to secure sponsorships. An analysis of the role sheets will provide the key insights into determining who these individuals should be. All areas of expertise required by the role sheets should be represented on the acquisition team whenever possible.

The Sponsorship Acquisition Manager is the key sponsorship acquisition team member. This person will have the ultimate responsibility for organizing, funding, and promoting your program. The person most capable of ensuring the completion of these tasks should be selected as Sponsorship Acquisition Manager. He or she should understand the sponsorship and the key issues involved, and have great customer service skills. Do not let concerns about what department will get the credit detract from selecting the best candidate for Sponsorship Acquisition Manager.

With the acquisition team in place, the following tasks should occur immediately:

- Develop an organized sponsorship filing system
- Create an acquisition timeline
- Assign individuals responsibility for different portions of acquisition

---

- Sponsorship Acquisition Manager has technical expertise and proposal management/writing experience.
- Composite technical expertise of team addresses all areas of the Role Sheets
- Proposal team includes:

  People who will actually help deliver the sponsor's benefits
  Experienced proposal writers
  Word processing/graphics support
  Professional advisors (accounting, legal, marketing, sponsorship and finance)

Figure 3-2. Characteristics of the Acquisition Team.

Getting Organized

Developing an organized sponsorship filing system is one of the first tasks that the acquisition team must complete when preparing to develop a sponsorship program. If you want your sponsorship program to be successful, you must develop a sponsorship filing system.

Maintaining a sponsorship filing system is an effective way, in a short period of time to assemble a large amount of materials needed for sponsorship acquisition. The filing system will make your sponsorship information accessible to you and your team at a moments notice, and provide necessary information to prepare agreements and other paper work.

On the following page is an example of a sponsorship filing system. It represents a short list of possible files that will make the development and expansion of your program less pain-staking and tedious. By no means is this list inclusive, feel free to add files as the need arises.

Sponsorship Filing System

The sponsorship program filing system should include folders for:

Preparation
1. Organizational chart
2. Team roles and expected results
3. Policies and procedures
4. Bookkeeping system
5. Sponsorship acquisition budget

Property Analysis
1. Audience demographics for each sponsorship opportunity
2. Salable assets for each sponsorship opportunity

Sponsorship Blueprint Design
1. Up-to-date property plan

Sponsor Analysis
1. Sponsor target list
2. Sponsor's active role in sponsorship opportunity
3. Sponsorship categories
4. Distribution of benefits

Property Marketing
1. Research data on current and new product launches

Sponsor Recruitment
1. Sponsorship opportunity letter
2. Sponsorship opportunity brochure
3. Rejection letters

Proposals
1. Proposal boilerplate
2. Winning proposals
3. Non-sponsored proposals
4. Sample proposals from other properties

Sponsorship In Action
1. Files for current and past sponsors

Step 5.   *Document* policies and procedures

Any successful sponsorship program depends in part on the commitment of the organization to be competitive and clear policies and procedures. Many properties operate without clear policies and procedures which maximize the dynamics and personalities of staff, board and committee members. Policies will engage the appropriate people in the sponsorship efforts, which will increase profitability. Here are some of the questions that will help you build your governance:

1. How will you allocate responsibilities internally?
2. What are the sponsor obligations?
3. Who will make sales calls?
4. What sponsorship opportunities are for sale?
5. What is your recruitment period?
6. When is the budget set?
7. How do you track promotional consideration?
8. Who approves sponsorship deals?
9. How do you anticipate utilizing sponsorships?
10. What is the Board's commitment?
11. What is the standard sponsorship training progression for staff, Board members and volunteers?
12. Do you have limitations as to the sponsorship categories you will not accept?
13. What is your policy regarding outside consultants?

We have provided an example of a sponsorship policy on the next couple of pages. Although many of these document vary this example should provide a good basis for developing yours.

Example

TORONTO BOARD OF EDUCATION

SPONSORSHIP POLICY

The Toronto Board of Education believes that through mutually beneficial partnerships that the overall quality of life in the educational system can be enhanced, community relationships can be strengthened, and efficiencies in time and resources can be achieved.

The Toronto Board of Education believes that collaboration with corporate america in the design and delivery of sponsorship programs will provide an enhanced and more relevant education for all students. The board believes the partnership may include, but not limited to the following sponsorships:

Athletic fields
Benefits
Celebrations
Conferences
Community Schools
Graduations
Concerts
Dances
Entrepreneur Programs
Film Festivals
Interscholastic sports
Social clubs
Special Programs

The Board and all its schools may enter into partnership with business and industry. The partnership shall:

1. meet identified educational or extra-curricula need;
2. be mutually beneficial; and
3. avoid commercialization.

The sponsoring company should

1. Not engage the Board in what would appear to be either side of a contentious political, moral or social issue; and

2. Demonstrate practices that represent those of concerned citizen, e.g., safety and health procedures, and environmental issues and equity.

DEFINITIONS

1. Sponsorship

Cash, products or services in-exchange for acknowledgment with the context of this policy.

SPONSORSHIPS

1. Conditions of Sponsorship

Prior to entering into any sponsorship agreement, the participating school (s), area, or Board staff shall clearly determine the sponsor's expectations.

The following information shall be collected in order to determine a potential sponsor's eligibility:

(a) the nature and product or service of the sponsor;
(b) information about the sponsor's history;
(c) reason for sponsor's interest in the Board;
(d) the activity or event around which the sponsor wishes to create a sponsorship agreement; and
(e) representatives of the firm with whom the Board and staff will work, including any outside advertising or communications agency.

2. Terms of Sponsorship Agreement

The following details shall be documented prior to establishing a sponsorship agreement:

(a) the duration of the agreement;
(b) the roles, responsibilities and rights of sponsor; and
(c) the outcome of the sponsorship.

3. Approval of Sponsorship

School based agreements shall be by the principal in consultation with parents and the superintendent of schools.

Area agreements shall be approved by the superintendent of schools.

Regional agreements shall be approved by Administrative Council.

System agreements require Board approval.

4. Financial Reports

Financial reports are to be submitted to the Superintendent of Business, or designee.

Step 6. *Set* your budget

One of the most difficult situations you will face annually is sponsorship budgeting. It's a function that requires you to predict what you'll need, what it will cost and the income to be realized. The most frequently asked question in sponsorship budgeting is how much?

The real question should be what are the methods for setting sponsorship budgets? There are five different ways to establish a sponsorship budget.

1. **"Percent of Sales"**: This is the most often used method. If you sell more sponsorships, you'll invest more into acquisition. This is literally putting the cart before the horse.

2. **"Percent of Income"**: This is a more sensible method, but is just as limiting. Under this method, acquisition seems to be tied to its return on investment, but again it puts the horse in the wrong place.

3. **"Matching the competition"**: Another budgeting option. Here, properties estimate what other properties are investing and matches that. The problem with this method is that it keeps you evenly paced with the competition and prevents you from gaining on them.

4. **"Combination"**: This method is a combination of the first and third. It's called "keep pace" method. It calls for your property to invest an amount proportionally equal to your competitions sales to promotion ratio. Thus, if your competitor invests 5% on sponsorship acquisition you do the same.

5. **"Task Oriented"**: The most sophisticated method. As implied, the object is to achieve a task or goal. When we apply this method to your program, you start with a list of all the promotional tactics that would advance your communication strategy, citing the task it is intended to achieve. Some call this a "wish list", or "promotional menu."

   We then prioritize the items on the list and assign costs to each. When this is done, determine what is essential, what can be reduced, what can be postponed and what can be eliminated. Now you are ready to formulate a sponsorship budget based on what your property can afford to invest.

   The benefit of this method is that it lets promotion be the driving force for your overall sponsorship acquisition rather than the "necessary expense" as some may view it.

Sponsorship Program
Sample Budget

Use this format only as a suggested guide to laying out your sponsorship budget columns and categories. Type your sponsorship budget on a separate sheet, itemizing whatever is indicated. Remember as your sponsorships increase your labor costs increase.

CATEGORIES	$AMOUNT
Sponsorship Preparation	**$8,582.25**
IEG Legal Guide to Sponsorship	$89
IEG Sponsordisk	$895
Sponsorship Training Manuals 10@ $99.95	$999.50
Bookkeeping Register	$10
Sponsorship Seminar 2 @ $99.95	$199.75
File Cabinet	$39
Property Letterhead & Envelopes	$150
Business Cards (Acquisition Team)	$200
Preparation 300hrs @ $20	*$6,000*
Property Analysis	**$800**
Analysis 40hrs @ $20	*$800*
Sponsorship Blueprint Design	**$2,000**
Design 100hrs @ $20	*$2,000*
Property Marketing	**$5,900**
Cycle Mailings $50 per 1,000	$150
IEG Conference	$2,500
Display Ad (Sponsorship Connection)	$250
Marketing 150@$20	*$3,000*
Sponsor Analysis	**$2,000**
Analysis 100hrs @ $20	*$2,000*

Sponsor Recruitment   **$19,200**
Telephone $3,600
Sponsorship Opportunity Brochure $1,600
Travel (Site Visits) $7,000
Recruitment 350hrs @ $20   *$7,000*

Proposal Development   **$100,000**
Packaging $40,000
Development 300hrs @ $20   *$60,000*

Execute Sponsorship   **$4,700**
Legal $2,000
Monthly Sponsor Reports $300
Execution 120hrs @ $20   *$2,400*

TOTAL BUDGET $143,182.25

Step 7.   *Set-up* your tax-saving bookkeeping system

One of the most important, but least understood or appreciated aspects of any sponsorship program is its bookkeeping or accounting system. And, because very few properties know much about the reasons for a sponsorship bookkeeping system, most people are frightened by the thought of the work involved in setting up such a system, and the drudgery of daily maintenance.

There's really nothing complicated about sponsorship bookkeeping, it's as simple as keeping a daily diary and/or maintaining your checkbook. At the bottom line, it's simply a matter of recording your cash, products or services-incoming promotional consideration and keeping a record of the money you spend.

So, the first thing you need to do is open a sponsorship account for your promotional consideration. Generally, this is simply a matter of asking the new accounts teller at your bank for a business account registration fee, send it in to the appropriate commissioner, and from there, open your new sponsorship account- complete with imprinted checks.

Drop by a local stationary store and pick up loose leaf notebook, and a supply of paper. Pick up a supply of index tabs at the same time—to separate the months of accountability for each sponsorship package you sell.

You want to make it as simple as possible, while at the same time keep it efficient - here's what you do and how to do it.

On the first page in your notebook, write on the top line and in the middle of the page: Monday, January 1, 1999 the day you officially start your sponsorship opportunity…Then, as your sponsorship cash, products or services come in by mail just jot down starting on the left side of the page, the amount you received-dash-for what-from whom, and their address. The page might look like this:

Monday --- January 1, 1999

$VALUE	PROMOTIONAL CONSIDERATION (Cash, Products and Services)
$2,500	Cash---Adidas Inc.
$500	Printing----Safeco Insurance Co.
$5,000	300 Cases of Spring Water---Spring Mountain

TOTAL INCOME: $8,000   **EXPENSES: 0**

That's all there is to it, and boiling it all down, it amounts to recording what you receive and what you spend. The next entry, immediately under that first day's entry might look like this:

$8500 Deposit

$3   Bookkeeping register

$189   How To Produce Millions In Corporate Sponsorship Manual (2 copies)

TOTAL INCOME $0   **EXPENSES $192**   **DEPOSIT $8,500**

And then, carry on with this recording of the promotional consideration you receive and spend each day with similar entries for each day of the week for every day, Monday thru Saturday for each week. It's simple, uncomplicated, and a positive record of your sponsorship activity.

Then at the end of the each month, transfer this activity information to one of the low cost bookkeeping registers that your tax consultant and accountant can work from. These people won't work from your daily diary, and will not transfer the information you record to a formal bookkeeping register without charging you a small fortune. It's not that big of a job, and if you do it after the close of business on the last day of the month, it will take at the most a few minutes. Then of course, when you're ready to do your annual report, you simply give your bookkeeping to your accountant, and you're home free.

The bookkeeping register can be a simple columnar notebook. All you need is some sort of note book with a number of columns marked off, a title written at the top of each column, and a record of the money received for each day relative to the sponsorship package each column represents. Then at the end of each month, you can simply add the totals from each column and you'll instantly know how much cash, products, and services you took in from each sponsor.

Beyond the date column, will be your record of expenses or money spent. Again, you should title each of the columns you'll be entering figures into, and then record your expenditures for items falling into those categories. Then at the end of each month, it's a simple matter to add the total from each column and know exactly where you stand relative to profit and loss - how much promotional consideration you took in compared to how much you spent.

Bookkeeping and/or accounting is very simple and should not scare you. Just keep it simple, and up-to-date.

Step 8.   *Train* members of your staff, Board of Directors and volunteers

In today's hectic sponsorship climate, it's often difficult for properties to curve out time for self-improvement. All of us in the industry can benefit from taking stock in ourselves, setting sponsorship goals, and building your knowledge, skills and abilities. Single point lessons can help staff, Board members and volunteers assess their strengths and weaknesses and develop the competencies needed for professional growth.

HERE'S YOUR ROAD TO SUCCESS

The single point lessons in this section were developed based on the needs of properties, as expressed through surveys, personal observation, consultation with properties, input form seminar participants and analysis of position specification. Topics were carefully designed to address the most pressing issues and challenges facing staff and property managers. These single point lessons will be continually reviewed to ensure that properties have access to the latest and most relevant information.

Sponsorship Acquisition Professionals will learn:

Finance
- How To Calculate Return On Investment (ROI)

Marketing
- Basics of Promotion Advertising
- How To Write Press Releases
- The Art of Salesmanship
- "The 9 Rules of Branding"
- Tips on Getting Celebrity Endorsements
- 10 Steps To Success In Sponsorship Recruitment

Legal
- The Sponsorship Code
- Sponsorship Tax Laws
- Facts about Copyrights
- How To Copyright What You Wrote

Acquisition
- Systems Approach To Sponsorship Acquisition

8.1   How To Calculate Return On Investment (ROI)

Everyone in the sponsorship industry should have a clear understanding of Return on Investment (ROI) as it applies to various sponsorship packages. The question: "How do these benefits add value to an organization's bottom line?" This needs to be answered before any sponsor will invest any money in your property.

Calculation of ROI

There are two formulas for calculating how much a certain investment will return to a sponsor's bottom line. These two are typically called the benefit-to-cost ratio and the Return on Investment (ROI):

$$BCR = \frac{Program\ Benefits}{Program\ Cost} \qquad ROI\ (\%) = \frac{Net\ Program \times 100}{Program\ Costs}$$

The BCR utilizes the total benefits and costs, whereas the ROI uses only the net benefits (total less costs). For example, if a certain sponsorship proposal provides benefits of $1,000,000 and costs $200,000, then the BCR is:

$$BCR = \frac{\$1,000,000}{\$200,000} = 5/5\text{-}1$$

That is, for every $1 invested, $5 in benefits is returned. This is called a "5 to 1" investment. The net benefit in this example is $800,000 ($1,000,000 - $200,000), so the ROI calculation is:

$$ROI\ (\%) = \frac{\$800,000 \times 100}{\$200,000} = 400\%$$

This means that for each $1 invested, there is a $4 return in net benefits. Note that benefits and costs are usually calculated for each proposal.

8.2   Basics of Promotion Advertising

Promotion advertising differs significantly from consumer advertising. The latter is long-term in nature and aimed at giving customers reasons to buy. Promotion advertising is short-term. It pushes for the order by providing incentives, coupons, rebates, premiums and contests.

The usual medium for promotional advertising is print. Some big-budget advertisers use broadcast (radio & television) to get consumers to look for their promotion in their local newspaper.

As a rule, promotion advertising should be specific and should call only for the consumer to perform a desired action. Resist including extraneous points in the promotional material. Focus simply on the call to action.

For example your ad might ask readers to:

1) Redeem this coupon and save $2, or
2) Buy two packs and get the third FREE, or
3) Fill out the coupon and enter the sweepstakes to win $100,000, or
4) Buy two of the products and get a gift for $10.

Most promotions are price or value-added oriented campaigns. As such, it is imperative that when writing copy, the ad should appeal more to the wallet than emotion.

Final point: do not make your redemption procedure complicated or confusing. Avoid having more than one theme offer wherein the consumer is forced to use math in order to determine which ones save him/her more money. Your task is to make it easy for the consumer. Avoid having to make them decide.

8.3   How To Write Press Releases

The word "Press Release" seems to scare most properties to death. On top of that –
not many properties take the time to even think of writing their own Press Release. We
hope this brief single point lesson helps to clear up some of the mysteries surrounding
this simple form of marketing.

The first thing you have to remember is that a "Press Release" is a "news" item. It needs
to inform people, **NOT** sell them something. For example, you are reading this lesson
because you want to learn something that will BENEFIT you. You aren't reading it so
you can buy something else. If money is the driving force of your sponsorship
program—your won't go far. Your main goals should be in pleasing your customers,
providing them with a quality product and exceptional service greater than their fee. The
trick is to do all this while making money.

Your customers don't care what mountains you had to climb, what seas you had to
cross or what tribe of people you had to learn the ways to create the secret formula.
Instead they want to know WHAT the secret formula is. Get the idea?

Your property profile, cover letter, sponsorship brochure, sale circulars sells your
sponsorship opportunity. A Press Release informs others about your property. Instead
of the main objective being to sell your property and have your prospects issue checks,
a Press Release informs the customer exactly how your property will benefit them. This
must be conveyed in the form of a "newsworthy" Press Release.

The following is a sample of a typical Press Release for our publishing services:

Letterhead

For Immediate Release

Date: March 21,
1997

For more information Contact:
Renee Crenshaw
215 477-1509

Philadelphia, Pa—so many people are entering home-based business these days, but so many are
getting ripped-off by a bunch of hype. People are promised untold riches in a short period of time. The
hype ads play with their emotions by making them believe it's so easy to make money through home-
based businesses. It's sad.

However, a new audio cassette has just been released to help solve these problems for the average
person. For the first time in history—a real resource has been developed . It's unbelievable. Without trying
to sell you anything else, you can get this audio series for only $39.95 a price anyone can afford.
Only available from International Money Group, 5128 Ogden St., Philadelphia, Pa 19139.

###

As you can see, this is a short, but sweet Press Release however, you should be able to see the "newsworthiness" in it. The main focus is on the fact that most people get ripped-off when they start their first home-based business. The solution to this problem is a new audio cassette series that is available for the first time in history. The sell is slowly led into because the reader will naturally want to get their hands on this one. It doesn't ask for money it only tells the reader how to get a copy if they want one.

Here's the greatest test for a real press release. Since your final sales pitch is included in the last paragraph read the Press Release out loud. Would it still be worth reading WITHOUT your sales pitch? If so, it's probably a Press Release.

Press Releases come in many forms due to the sponsorship opportunity you are writing about. However, the basic rule of thumb still applies. If you've never wrote one before it may be a little difficult. Don't despair. Grab the latest daily newspaper and read some of their informational articles. Notice how each article is written and pattern yours after the same format. After you do a few of them, you'll be able to "get the picture."

When your Press Release is written to your satisfaction, the proper way to submit a news release to the publisher is listed below:

- Type it on a typewriter or computer.
- Double space and keep type not longer than two 81/2 x11 pages.
- Put your name, address and page number at the top of each page.
- Write the words "For Immediate Release." at the top.

If you are only sending the press release to one publication tell them it's a first run."

8.4   The Art of Salesmanship

This is were it gets fun and interesting. Remember going in, that you must be convinced of the value of your offer, before you can expect a like return from your prospective sponsor. The most prevalent failure factors are (1) being afraid to ask and (2) viewing the sale as an all or nothing proposition. Selling is all strategy. It's finding the middle ground. It's negotiations and compromises. The odds are slim that everything will go according to your plan. Don't get angry or frustrated. All sponsorship solicitors face rejection, even the most seasoned veterans. The successful individual will be the most prepared.

Selling rules and strategies

- Successful sponsorship solicitors are not "good talkers" or "fast talkers." The opposite is true; they are good listeners.

- The sponsorship solicitor does not present the sponsorship opportunity to the sponsor until the salesperson learns what the sponsor's objectives, needs, problems (or all three) are.

- The sponsorship solicitor never begins the sales call with a presentation, because that establishes a one-way communication. The salesperson needs a dialogue so that he or she can develop a consultative approach to helping the sponsor.

- The successful sponsorship solicitor present only the benefits of the sponsorship opportunity that relates to the sponsor's priorities and objectives.

- The successful sponsorship solicitors does not try to close the sale after every opportunity. He or she closes only after it's clear that the sponsorship opportunity meets the client's needs.

- The successful sponsorship solicitor does not believe that the sponsor relationship ends with the sale. In fact, the sponsor relationship begins with the sale.

- The sponsorship solicitor's goal is to develop beyond being simply a sales rep and grow into being a sustaining resource for all sponsors.

The role of the sponsorship solicitor's has dramatically changed over the years. The salesperson was a presenter of information. The sponsorship opportunity was more important than the sponsor. Now the concept of need-benefit selling has developed. Sponsorship solicitors work to find sponsor needs and then show how the sponsorship opportunity fulfilled those needs.

8.5 "The 9 Rules of Branding"

For over 100 years the characteristics of brand behavior have remained constant. In aggregate, together these characteristics form what we call, "The 9 Rules of Branding," principles that remain true regardless of the market forces or social economic changes.

The 9 Rules of Branding

(1) Brands Represent Clear Value(s)

Consumers have come to see leading brands as a hallmark of product quality, safety and consistency and, as a result, a "value" on several levels. While private labels are often seen as offering a price value, and even second or third brands are seen as being safe, leading brands represent multi-dimensional sets of values to the consumer.

(2) Brands Communicate an Unambiguous Message to the consumer

Whatever the value proposition(s) of the brand, it or they are communicated clearly to the consumer. Great brands become great brands because their value is clearly understood. Any number of good product and/or service offerings fail not because of any inherent weaknesses in the offering, but because of the brands ability to communicate clearly with consumers.

(3) Brands Differentiate Offerings

Brands enable consumers to differentiate and negotiate their way through the sometimes perilous waters of product/service proliferation. Faced with excessive choice, consumers often choose not to choose, unless there is a vehicle available to facilitate what they believe is an informed choice. Often the vehicle is a brand name.

(4) Brands Make a Promise to the Consumer

A brand is a promise offered by a manufacturer to the consumer, and a product or service is nothing more or less than evidence of the truthfulness of that promise. If a brand breaks faith with the consumer just once, its ability to make promises over time will be eliminated.

(5) Brands Innovate

A great deal has been written over the past decade about the ability of private label products to deliver value, but little is ever written about their ability to bring true innovation to the market. Given the advances in food technology, it is relatively easy to either clone a product or, once having clone the formula, to improve on one or two critical elements of the formula. Put another way, once you have the recipe for a chocolate chip cookie it's relatively simple to add more chips, a higher grade of chocolate or make the cookies larger.

(6) Brands Build Loyalty

Loyalty requires an object one must be loyal to someone or something. Since the concept of brands can be extended to anything or anyone who produces products, offer them for sale or provides a service, brands can build loyalty toward a retail store, a chain, a channel and, obviously, a manufacturer. The ability to build brand loyalty not only impacts product or service trial but repeat business as well.

(7) Brand Power Is Transferable

Brand franchises are transferable (within limits) to other brands and even to unrelated goods, services and experiences. The Coca-Cola brand is only one of dozens that has been transferred to a clothing line. The Harley-Davidson brand has been extended to a host of lifestyle products, including bars and restaurants. In fact, the list of transferable brand equity is virtually endless, although not all these transfers benefit the brand long term.

(8) Brands Endure

The clearest strength of great brands is their ability to maintain their vitality over time, even after their initial applications have lapsed. This strength allows the brand value to survive well past the product to which it was initially attached.

(9) Brands Are Not Created Equal

Most products or services carry a brand but not all brands carry the same weight in the consumer's mind. That's because some brands are nothing more than a label and a name. They fail to meet one or more of the criteria outlined on this list and are, therefore, less effective in terms of their ability to deliver value.

8.6   Tips on Getting Celebrity Endorsements

Celebrity endorsements can encourage others in the community to join in. These endorsements often help get better media coverage and makes your sponsorship opportunity high profile.

Getting a celebrity or public figure to agree to publicly endorse your property can be a challenge. However, don't be dismayed if you can't get Jim Carey, Michael Jordan or The Backstreet Boys to attend your function. It is often more effective to get an endorsement of a local celebrity or public figure. For example, your local television sportscaster can give a big boost to your properties efforts.

So whether you are going for Michael Jordan or your local TV weather luminary, the following 3 steps will help you plan your approach and get the celebrity you target to endorse your property.

Step 1. Prepare yourself

1. *Be persistent* -- The bigger the celebrity the more gatekeepers they will have. Be prepared to make multiple calls and explain the purpose of your call before you get through to the celebrity or the manager who can make a commitment.

2. *Be tough skinned* – Celebrities and their agents are busy people. They often use a cut-to-the chase approach that seems abrupt and even rude.

3. *Be organized* – Prepare a pitch that is precise and specific.

4. *Follow-up* – Prepare a follow up letter and packet of information about your property.

5. *Go directly to the source* – If the celebrity you want to contact is local, try to schedule a face-to-face meeting. Contact the television station, studio etc., and try to schedule a meeting.

6. *Be enthusiastic* – Even though you may have to make your pitch several times to various managers, secretaries and personal assistants working for the celebrity, maintain your enthusiasm about your solicitation. Let them know that the participation of the celebrity they work for is an important part of helping to reach your goals and the celebrity will be recognized.

7. *Be flexible* – If the celebrity can't meet your initial request, have several alternatives you can propose. For example:

- If the celebrity can't attend your event, ask them to send a telegram or letter of support.

- If the celebrity can't record a Public Service Announcement (PSA), ask them if you can use a photo and statement of support in your campaign literature.

8. *Be prepared* – Make sure your first experience with a celebrity is a successful and pleasant one. If the celebrity is attending a press conference or other public event, assign someone in your group as a liaison. The person will make sure the celebrity or the agent has all of the details related to the event, he/she will make any special arrangements the celebrity may require and most importantly, cater to the celebrities ego.

Step 2. Identify the right celebrity
The following tips will help you identify which celebrity is right for your property.

Decide on the type of celebrity you think will be the most effective in promoting the campaign in your community. Is there a natural link between the celebrity and the campaign (i.e. former school employee, known for supporting education, appeared at other education-related events, etc.)? Do you want your campaign associated with a Sports star? Movie actor? Television personality? Also determine whether you will use a local celebrity or if you try to get someone with national recognition. An important consideration when making this determination is whether you or someone you know has a personal contact with a celebrity. This contact will make it easier to get through to the celebrity and get their support.

Step 3. Contact the celebrity
Most celebrities have a publicist or agent. Often you can find out who the celebrity's agent or publicist is by contacting the television station on which they appear, sports team they play for, newspaper they appear in, record label they record for, publisher they write for, etc. Below are some of the resources you may find helpful in contacting celebrities:

Film Actors

Screen Actors Guild (SAG) – The Screen Actors Guild is an AFL-CIO union representing actors who appear in film.

Television Performers

American Federation of Television and Radio Artists, AFL-CIO (AFTRA) – represents people who perform on television and radio. This includes actors, television and radio news reporters and anchors, and other personalities. To identify the agent or publicist of a television or radio artist contact the national office of AFTRA.

Musicians

American Federation of Musicians, AFL-CIO (AFM) – AFM represents many of the top recording and performing musicians and singers in the country. You can get the name and number of a performers agent through the AFM local which the performer belongs. Most of the big name performers belong to AFM locals in New York and Los Angeles. Contact the national office for the phone number of these and other AFM locals.

Sports

Major League Baseball Players Associations – This is an independent union representing Major League Baseball players.

Federation of Professional Athlete – This union represents football players in the National Football League. To get information on the player's agent, contact the Research Department at the Federations national office in Washington D.C.

National Basketball Players Association (NBA Players Association) – This union represents professional basketball players. You can get the name and phone number of a players agent by contacting the national office.

8.7   Steps To Success In Sponsorship Recruitment

Here are seven steps that will assure your success:

1. **Be a Goal Setter.** What do you want to accomplish? Do you want to produce millions in corporate sponsorship? Do you want to secure a television sponsor? You can have whatever you want, but you must want it enough to do what it takes to get it. Whatever your goal, write it down and set a target date for reaching it. Divide the time period into blocks of achievement that are reachable. Work consistently toward accomplishing your goal, each day, each week, each month what you set out to do. Little is ever accomplished without defined goals.

2. **Be a list maker.** Each evening list all the things you want to get done the following day. That gives you an organized approach to each day. As each task is finished, mark it off your list. It is amazing how much gets done when one works with a "things-to-do" list. Also, have a notebook listing appointments, potential sponsors, repeat sponsors, and referrals, and keep it with you at all times. You will be adding to it constantly.

3. **Be enthusiastic.** Enthusiasm is the high-octane "fuel" that sponsorship acquisition professionals run on. Enthusiasm generates its own energy. Energy and good health are synonymous with busy, happy people who are achieving.

4. **Recognize that the magic word in sponsorship recruitment is "ask."** In sponsorship recruitment, we don't wait until a sponsor comes to us. We create our own sponsorship revenue by asking for it. Ask for the sponsorship, then you will close the deals. Ask for referrals, have a full list of potential sponsors. Be quietly, yet firmly aggressive.

5. **Expect No's.** Realize that no's are not personal. In recruitment, as perhaps nowhere else, the law of averages work. Every no gets you closer to a yes. Keep track of the ratio. It will help improve your techniques. Are you getting 10 no's to one yes? Is your ratio five to one? Remember, a yes is your income. Also it is simply a stall for more time to think. It may be a request for more information about your property. What your sponsor is actually buying is assurance. Assure them by your helpful attitude and your complete honestly, that what you want is best for them. They will most likely respect you and do business with you.

6. **Schedule time wisely.** A schedule is the roadmap by which sponsorship acquisition professionals travel. It takes the frustration out of the day. It assures that the necessary things get done and get done on time. Plan your work then work your plan.

7. **Be positive in your attitude.** Success in sponsorship sales, as in all areas of life is 90% percent attitude and 10% aptitude. All of us must work on developing constructive thinking. I am proud to be a sponsorship acquisition professional. Sales make the wheels of our economy turn. Without sponsorship acquisition professionals, properties would be paralyzed.

8.8   Sponsorship Code

International Money Group's intention is to set some basic guidelines for good practice and fairness in sponsorship so that sponsorship may play its proper role. It is also designed to serve as an interpretative aid for all parties in the classification of uncertainties arising under the sponsorship.

SCOPE OF THE CODE
The code applies to all sponsorship related to corporate image, brands, products, service activities or events of any kind.

BASIC PRINCIPLES

A. All sponsorship should be honest, truthful, legal and conform to the accepted principles of fair competition in business.

B. The terms and conduct of sponsorship should be based upon principles of fairness and good faith between both parties.

C. The sponsorship should be based on contractual obligations between both parties. Sponsorship should be acknowledged and should not be misleading.

D. All categories of sponsors who are legally allowed to conduct business are free to sponsor any activity, event or programme of any kind and to define a set of sponsorship objectives, provided that such sponsorship is consistent with the principles of fairness set in this code.

RULES

Clarity and Accuracy
Rule #1
Sponsorship and all related communications should be subject to the principle of clarity and accuracy with respect to all persons and organizations taking part in the sponsorship and to any rights or other privileges granted to the sponsor.

Imitation and Confusion
Rule #2
Sponsors and sponsored parties, as well as other parties involved in a given sponsorship, should avoid imitation of the representation of other sponsorships where imitation might mislead or generate confusion, even if applied to non-competitive products, companies or events.

Parties to the Sponsorship
Rule #3

The sponsor should take particular care and safeguard the inherent artistic, cultural, sporting or other content of the sponsored activity or organization and should avoid any abuse of its position which would damage the identity, dignity, or reputation of the sponsored party.

The sponsored party should never obscure, deform or impugn the image or trademarks of the sponsor, nor should it jeopardize the goodwill or public appreciation they have already earned.

The Sponsorship Audience
Rule #4

The audience should be clearly informed of the existence of a sponsorship with respect to a particular event, activity or programme or person and the sponsor's message should not deliberately offend the audience's religious, political or social convictions.

Children and Young People
Rule #5

Sponsorship addressed to or likely to influence children or young people should not be framed so as to take advantage of their youth or lack of experience. Furthermore, such sponsorship should not be framed so as to harm children or young people mentally, morally or physically, nor to stain their sense of loyalty to their parents and guardians.

Multiple Sponsorship
Rule #6

Where the activity or event requires or allows multiple sponsors, the individual contracts and agreements should clearly set out (and inform all sponsors of) the respective rights, limits and obligations of each sponsor. The sponsored party should be aware of the importance of keeping an appropriate balance between sponsors.

In particular, each member of the pool of sponsors should respect the defined sponsorship fields and the allotted communication tasks, abstaining from any interference that might unfairly alter the balance between the contribution of each sponsor.

The sponsored party should inform any possible future sponsors of any sponsors already a party to the sponsorship. The sponsored party shall not accept a new sponsor without the approval of sponsors who are already contractual parties to the sponsorship.

Television, Radio and Cinema
Rule #7
The content and scheduling of sponsored programmes should not be influenced by the sponsor so as to abrogate the responsibility, autonomy or editorial independence of the broadcaster or programme producer.

Sponsored programmes should be identified as such by display of the sponsor's name and/or logo at the beginning and/or end of programme.

Care should be taken to ensure that there is no confusion between sponsorship of an event or activity and the television, radio or cinema transmission of that event or activity.

8.9 Sponsorship Tax Laws

On August 6, 1997, President Clinton signed into law the Taxpayer Relief Act of 1997. Along with hundreds of other provisions, the new law addresses the federal income tax treatment of corporate sponsorship income received by non-profit organizations. The new law allows tax-exempt the activity of soliciting and receiving *qualified sponsorship payments.*

A *qualified sponsorship payment* is designated as any payment made by any individual or entity engaged in a trade or business where there is no arrangement or expectation that the sponsor will receive any substantial return benefit other than the use or acknowledgment of the sponsor's name, logo, and product lines in connection with the activities of the tax-exempt organization that receives the payment.

Acknowledgments
Material that includes the following constitutes an acknowledgment, which is not subject to IRS taxation:

- Sponsor logos and slogans that do not contain comparative or qualitative descriptions of the sponsor's products, services, facilities, or company.
- Sponsor locations or telephone numbers.
- Value-neutral descriptions, including displays or visual depiction's.
- Sponsor brand or trade names.
- Product or service listings.
- Payments contingent on the mere occurrence of an event.

Advertising
Material that includes the following constitutes advertising and may be taxed by the IRS:

- Qualitative or comparative language distinguishing a sponsor's products from its competitors.
- Price information or other indications of savings or value associated with a product or service.
- A call to action.
- An endorsement.
- An inducement to buy, sell, rent, or lease the sponsor's product or service.
- Payments that are contingent on broadcast ratings or attendance at an event.

8.10 Facts about Copyrights

Copyright is a widely misunderstood concept. The fact is, everything you've ever written, from your school notes to family bulletins, is yours, and unless you coped it from a copyrighted source, you own the copyright. This simple legal principle is accepted in most free-world countries, but it's almost useless to you in a court of law without some sort of proof.

The simplest way to assert copyright in all your sponsorship materials is to print © Your Name, Year. You'll notice we use the notification on our material. You can protect your copyright cheaply, and with a high degree of protection, by sealing the item to be copyrighted in a tamper-proof envelope, stamping the envelope over any point where the envelope could be opened, having the postal clerk postmark the stamps over the seal points, and mailing it back to yourself.

Label the envelope for future reference, and if you can, smudge the fresh postmark ink so there's a gray blotch between stamp and envelope. It can be scrutinized in court for tampering, and any half-decent forensic scientist will be able to shoot down any zealous attorney who tries to prove you faked it. You can copyright whole books this way for under $4.00.

8.11 How To Copyright What You Wrote

If you are the author, you can copyright books, poems, directories, leaflets, pamphlets, newsletters and bulletins. In essence you can copyright almost anything you write or draw as long as you comply with the following procedures:

1. Produce copies with copyright notice

Produce the work in copies by printing or other means of reproduction. All copies must bear a copyright notice in the required form and as a general rule, the copyright notice should consist of three elements.

   a. The word "copyright", the abbreviation "copy", or the symbol printed within the circle (©).
   b. The name of the copyright owners.
   c. The year of copyright.

These elements should appear together on the copies

Example: Copyright 1964 John Smith
Example: © 1964 John Smith

For a publication printed in a book form, the copyright notice should appear on the title page or the page immediately following. The "page" immediately following" is normally on the reverse side of the page bearing the title.

2. Publish the work

3. Register the claim with the copyright office

Promptly after publication, you should send the following materials to the Copyright Office.

   a. Application for Registration. (For books, booklets, reports etc.)
   b. Two copies of the edition of the work as published.
   c. Registration fee of $10. Do not send cash. Payment must be in the form of a money order, check, or bank draft, payable to the "Registry of Copyrights", send everything to: Registry of Copyrights, Library of Congress, Washington DC.

Step 9. Develop Acquisition Timeline

The following schedule is for sample purposes only. Actual schedule will vary with each property. Additional projects and requirements for completion are determined by the Sponsorship Acquisition Manager in conjunction with the Acquisition Team.

16 Months (Begin Sponsorship Acquisition)

1. Review the characteristics, knowledge, skill and ability of million dollar sponsorship producers.
2. Set-up your properties organizational structure.
3. Select acquisition team.
4. Document policies and procedures.
5. Set budget.
6. Secure equipment.

15 Months

1. Identify target market and customer profile.
2. Design property plan.
3. Conduct sponsor analysis.
4. Prepare sponsorship benefits and levels.
5. Come to terms with media.

13 Months

1. Recruit sponsors
2. Develop customized proposals.
3. Develop task flow chart.
4. Develop operating plan.

12 Months Prior

1. Continue sponsor recruitment.
2. Continue customized proposal development.

11 Months Prior

1. Continue sponsor recruitment.
2. Continue customized proposal development.

10 Months Prior

1. Continue sponsor recruitment.
2. Continue customized proposal development.
3. Determine volunteer requirements.
4. Establish criteria for local advertising and promotions.

9 Months Prior

1. Continue sponsor recruitment.
2. Continue customized proposal development.
3. Develop the sponsor status newsletter.
4. Establish friends of the property mailing.
5. Select local promotional materials.

8 Months Prior

1. Finalize sponsor recruitment.
2. Finalize customized proposal development.
3. Produce promotional materials.
4. Begin monthly meetings with team members.
5. Establish speakers bureau.

7 Months Prior (Execute Sponsorship)

1. Begin distribution of promotional materials.
2. Contact local media with coverage opportunities.
3. Distribute newsletter to sponsors, potential sponsors, team members, friends of the property, etc.
4. Develop local merchandising design, production and distribution plan.

6 Months Prior

1. Finalize sponsorship agreements.
2. Determine food needs (if applicable) and begin negotiations with caterers.

5 Months Prior

1. Begin production of souvenirs.
2. Develop volunteer registration and waiver forms.
3. Begin campaign for volunteers.
4. Determine parking and transportation needs.
5. Coordinate signage.

4 Months Prior

1. Determine venue signage opportunities and restrictions.
2. Review communication plan.
3. Review media center operations plan.
4. Continue volunteer solicitation.
5. Continue promotions.
6. Bid out souvenir program.

3 Months Prior

1. Begin media contacts.
2. Begin volunteer assignments.
3. Send out volunteer confirmations.
4. Contact sponsors for souvenir program.
5. Begin orientation of volunteer/temporary staff.

2 Months Prior

1. Confirm sponsor's attendance.
2. Confirm equipment needs.
3. Begin/update volunteer handbook.
4. Continue local promotions.
5. Establish weekly acquisition team meetings to review progress.

1 Month Prior

1. Review operations plans.
2. Produce souvenir booklet.
3. Inventory Celebration supplies.
4. Prepare media information.
5. Review sponsor registration and check-in process.

Month of Sponsorship Opportunity

1. Conduct volunteer orientation.
2. Setup and prepare site for Sponsors.
3. Complete volunteer assignments.
4. Contact media regarding media center.
5. Issue press releases.

Day of the Sponsorship Opportunity

1. Send out thank you letters.

Week After the Sponsorship Opportunity

1. Begin final reports.
2. Hold evaluation meeting.

Month Following the Sponsorship Opportunity

1. Renew current sponsors

The most comprehensive and affordable, step-b-step sponsorship recruitment training program on the market!

Sponsorship Recruitment 101-102™

Self-Study Course

Module Four

PROPERTY ANALYSIS

A Step-by-Step Guide To Identifying Your Salable Assets

Anthony B. Miles

With Renee Crenshaw

4.0 PROPERTY ANALYSIS

This internal analysis is based on three simple but powerful questions related to Anthony's "million dollar producers principles". Completing this module will help you understand your property and your role in it and identify opportunities to improve effectiveness.

Before approaching any sponsor you must be able to answer the following questions:

---

1. What is Our Property (Mission)?
2. Who is Our Target Audience?
3. What Is Our Plan?

"This module can keep you from heading for a fall"

Step 1.　　Define Properties Mission

This step helps you focus on the nature of your property—or mission—by asking a series of questions about the results your property seeks to achieve, its priorities, its strengths and weaknesses.

EXAMPLE

NATIONAL SPONSORSHIP OPPORTUNITY PLAN
PROPOSED MISSION STATEMENT
FOR THE
PARKS & RECREATION ASSOCIATION NETWORK

The Parks & Recreation Association Network is a nationwide network of independent and related associations that has been established to develop sponsorship and cause related marketing on the national level for the sole purpose of directly benefiting the economic environment for each association and its members.

Our mission is to create a national sponsorship opportunity that: serves as the anchor for innovative promotions, acts as a springboard toward economic self-reliance, mobilizes national community support for each independent association and unites all parties in the Parks & Recreation Association Network.

BACKGROUND

The independent program directors have identified a need to collaborate in order to leverage assets for the purpose of developing national sponsorship/promotion opportunities. As an initial step in that process, the recommendation was made to contract for assistance with the development of these opportunities. The goal is to produce additional funding for participating programs to meet each independent plan's objective.

OBJECTIVES

The key objectives of this sponsorship opportunity is to:

- Promote economic self-reliance.
- Improve the viability and awareness of the Parks & Recreation Association.
- Encourage collaboration among independent Parks & Recreation Associations.
- Maximize the use of volunteer resources.
- Exhibit consistent quality in management of promotion.
- Provide clear opportunities for recognition of sponsor volunteers and promotional consideration.
- Develop local marketing and promotional skills.
- Leverage promotional consideration with funds from other sources.

Step 2.   Identify your Properties Audience

Successful properties must constantly study their market, their competitors and the needs of their audience. Many small properties do not understand the need for market research and are frightened off by the term. They believe that only large properties continually carry out market research and often use sponsorship consultants to do this work. Small properties must also conduct market research. You may use sponsorship firms to do this work, or you may decide to carry out your own research.

Market research describes any method by which properties ascertain the size, characteristics and nature of their market.

How to conduct market research?
- Identify and list your objectives - define clear goals
- Decide what exactly you wish to know
- Gather relevant information about the market, your audience and your property
- Undertake research by means of questionnaire or interview, or combination of these methods
- Analyze the data
- Draw conclusions and make decisions
- Implement your decisions
- Follow your decisions

What can market research do for you? Market research can help to:
- Determine the demand for your property
- Identify target markets and customer profiles
- Analyze market trends
- Identify customer trends
- Forecast any changes in the market
- Determine whether your product/service is priced appropriately
- Determine whether your product/service is adequate or appropriate
- Identify new market opportunities

Three main factors that help you to identify target markets:
- geographic
- demographic
- psychological

<u>Factors identifying target markets</u>

Geographic factors

Location

- urban
- rural
- inter/outer suburbs
- distance from your sponsorship opportunity

Residence

- house
- apartment

Demographic factors

Age

- child
- teenager
- adult
- pensioner

Sex

- male
- female

Occupation

- blue collar
- white collar
- professional
- clerical
- trade

Income

- high
- middle
- low

Education

- secondary
- trade

Special Characteristics

- nationality
- religion
- race
- cultural background
- social class

Psychological factors

Lifestyle

- image
- preferences
- social mobility

Personal preferences

- hobbies
- interests

A. Marketing Budget

It is one thing to develop a marketing plan and another to implement it. The implementation stage of the marketing program will cost money, so you must be able to provide adequate funds. You will need to develop a marketing budget to match your marketing plan, and the marketing plan must reflect your properties objectives.

B. Evaluation of the marketing plan.

Implementing the plan and expending the funds will only be successful if an evaluation of the marketing plan shows the objectives by comparing the actual results with the proposed plan.

Step 3.   Analyze your Property

The following **28** questions found in the Sponsorship Activity Package on the next three pages will help you create a better overall picture your properties structure. It is intended to assist you in thinking through the key elements of your property. These questions will provide you with information needed to write a comprehensive property plan.

"This exercise will keep you from being out on a limb"

Sponsorship Learning Activity Package

PROPERTY ANALYSIS

SPONSORSHIP ACQUISITION TEAM ACTIVITY

PROPERTY LEARNING ACTIVITY PACKAGE

Property Project: 4-hour interactive acquisition team assignment

Goal: To provide a practical exercise which allows participants to apply the knowledge gathered in this manual, toward the skill of developing a property PLAN.

Objective: Given the 28 questions, analyze your property. Most of the information is contained in this manual, other necessary information you may have already developed. A certain amount of imagination and creativity are required to receive the full benefit of this exercise. Now read through the Sponsorship Learning Activity Package, paying close attention to every question. They contain the details needed to develop your property PLAN. Once you complete your review of the package, answer each question listed.

TASK #

_____ 1.   After thoroughly reviewing the questions found on the following pages, take a few minutes to discuss your property. Be certain that each acquisition team member has a clear understanding of the goals and objectives before continuing.

_____ 2.   Answer the questions 1-28.

1. What is the nature of your property?

2. What phase is your property in?

A. Start-up
B. Expansion
C. Developing New Properties
D. Strategic Partner or Partnerships

3. What is your properties corporate structure?

A. Sole proprietor
B. Partnership
C. Corporation
D. Not-for-profit
E. Other

4. Who is your sponsorship management team?

A. Sponsorship Acquisition Manager
B. Public Relations and Communications Manager
C. Marketing & Promotions Director
D. Sponsorship Acquisition Professional
E. Licensing & Strategic Partnerships
F. Corporate Identity and Graphic Communications

5. Who is your outside consultant team?

A. Legal (intellectual properties)
B. Accounting
C. Web Site Developer
D. Event Planner
E. Sponsorship Sales

6. What is your properties unique selling advantage? (Give details on why a company would what to sponsor your property).

7. What are your goals and objectives?

8. What would you like to achieve in annual sponsorship sales?

A. Year one $
B. Year two $
C. Year three $

9. How do you plan to achieve your annual sales goals?

10. What do you want to gain personally from your sponsorship acquisition efforts?

11. What other sponsorship opportunities will you develop?

12. How will your sponsors receive a return on their investment?

13. What is your demographic segment profile?

A   Business Consumer

B   Individual Consumer
         Age
         Income
         Sex
         Occupation
         Family size
         Culture
         Education

14. Who is your competition?

15. How is your competition promoting its property?

16. What are your properties plans?

A. Operational Plans
B. Sponsorship Staffing Plans
C. Marketing Plans
D. Sponsor Strategy

17. How much money do you need to operate your property for two years?

18. What will the money be used for?

19. What equipment do you need?

20. Will you/do you have sponsorship sales people? If yes, please indicate their territories, commissions, and salary structures.

21. How many salespeople will you have on staff during the next 24 months?

A. Outside
B. Inside

22. When does you sponsorship fiscal year end?

23. How will you be promoting your property?

24. How much will you spend on advertising in a typical year?

25. Who are your suppliers?

26. What is your market?

27. Do you have:

A. Sponsor Testimonials
B. Endorsements
C. Consumer surveys

28. Give some background on your management team?

4.1   Questions for the Sponsorship Acquisition Manager

1. **Fundraising Plan** - Is sponsorship an integral part or your fundraising planning.

2. **Decision-Making** - Do you have a clear decision-making process on sponsorship in your organization?

3. **Knowledge** - How much effort do you make to keep abreast of the most up to date sponsorship strategies.

4. **Staff** - Do you have experienced staff in-house to design, develop, implement and evaluate a comprehensive sponsorship program?

5. **Objectives** - Have you set clear objectives on the amount of sponsorship revenue?

6. **Fit** - Have you considered that your current sponsors may not be the right fit for your property?

7. **Evaluations** - Do you evaluate your properties sponsorships at all? Do you know what evaluation techniques are available? Do you know how your sponsorships are currently performing?

8. **Data** - Do you have sufficient data and knowledge in-house to access your properties demographics?

9. **Consultants** - Do you know the major sponsorship consultant in your area and have your fully evaluated their range of services?

Now that you understand the game of sponsorship and have responded to the questions above, you are ready to create your plan of action, which should be assembled around marketing and operations. Straight to the punch line. No games. No waiting. Here it is. The three secrets:

1. Set a goal
2. Make a plan
3. Follow the plan and reach the goal

The simplest thing anyone can do to achieve sponsorship success is make a plan and follow it. For properties small or large, planning and goal setting comes in the form of a property plan.

The most comprehensive and affordable, step-b-step sponsorship recruitment training program on the market!

Sponsorship Recruitment 101-102™

Self-Study Course

Module Five

BLUEPRINT DESIGN

A Step-by-Step Guide To Creating Your Functional Plan

Anthony B. Miles

With Renee Crenshaw

5.0 Property Blueprint Design

Given the rapid changes occurring in the sponsorship marketplace and the increasing levels of competition that all properties face, you can't afford to proceed blindly, hoping that hard work alone will be enough to make your sponsorship opportunities a success. To succeed, a property must have clearly defined objectives and a fully developed strategy for achieving them; in short, you need a property plan.

Far from reviewing a property plan as a luxury for large properties or something created to impress your staff, practitioners should see it for what it is - one of the most important tools a property can have. Just as an organization chart shows the working relationship of the people within a corporation, a property plan shows the purpose of the property and what it intends to accomplish. A good property plan helps give substance to an entrepreneurial vision, providing a mechanism that enables executives, managers, staff members and volunteers to function effectively.

When to use a property plan? Much like a Swiss Army knife, with its multitude of utensils, your property plan can serve many purposes. Among the times that your property plan should be of the greatest use to you when you're:

1. Starting your property
During the start-up stage of your sponsorship program, the existence of a sound property plan can mean the difference between success and failure. Rather than pursuing conflicting goals or allowing the program to develop haphazardly, you can use the plan to keep your program on track.

2. Expanding your property

Your plan can reduce risks involved in expanding your program. A plan is especially critical during the expansion phase since this is one of the most dangerous times for a property. If properties try to expand too quickly before mastering its current level of activity, the quality of its service to sponsors suffer. On the other hand if it waits too long, the market can be saturated with similar properties and funding may be lost.

3. Developing new sponsorship opportunities

For most properties the need to develop new opportunities is a fact of life brought about by the continuing challenge to satisfy their audience. To remain competitive, your program must be able to anticipate and respond to audiences changing needs. The way to accomplish this is by developing new opportunities and improving current ones.

Unless your property has a plan to guide it though, the chances of coming up with profitable ideas for new opportunities, modifications, or improvements are minimal. To make the most of your resources as your program grows, you must have a systematic plan for developing new opportunities and managing new ones.

4. Obtaining Strategic Partners

Corporate partners expect to see a property plan as a matter of course before they will give money or participate in a joint venture. Unless the plan can demonstrate they will earn a substantial return on their investment, the standard response is, "No go. No dough." This puts the burden on you to demonstrate through your plan that the investment will be worth their while.

5. Making management decisions

Perhaps the most valuable use of a property plan is making management decisions. By stating what the program intends to accomplish and assessing both internal and external environments, a property plan shows the "big picture". This gives sponsorship seekers a real advantage. Instead of operating in the dark or looking at just one aspect of sponsorship acquisition, they can consider it from all points of view and make a decision that is in the best interest of the program.

6. Maintaining control

Another key use of a property plan is a control device. Are goals being met? Did sponsorship package sales reach their target? Are attendance goals staying in line? Is the program doing what it set out to do?

You should be able to answer these questions and more by examining your property plan. Then by carefully rating your performance against your goals, you can determine if you're moving ahead or merely moving in place. If your method or strategy isn't working, or if you find that the program is going in a different direction, you can act quickly to bring things back in line or to chart a new course.

The plan

Once you've made up your mind about what kind of program to start and have done your preliminary research, you're ready to begin preparing your plan. Many of you may be tempted to skip this step, don't. The effort you put into it will be compensated for later when your program is operational. And the knowledge you gain from creating the finished, written plan will be invaluable.

Writing and putting together a "winning" property plan takes study, research and time, so don't try to do it all in just one or two days.

The easiest way to start is with a loose leaf notebook, plenty of paper, pencils, pencil sharpener, and several erasers. Once you get your mind "in gear" and begin thinking about your property plan, "10,000 thoughts and ideas per minute" will begin racing through your mind…So, it's a good idea when you aren't actually working on your property, to carry a pocket notebook and jot down those program ideas as they come to you—ideas for sales promotion, recruiting sponsors, and any other thoughts on how to operate and/or build your program.

Later, when you're actually working on your property plan, you can take out this "idea notebook" evaluate your ideas, rework them, refine them, and integrate them into the overall "big picture" of your property plan.

The best property plans for even the smallest properties run 25 to 30 pages or more, so you'll need to "title" each page and arrange the different aspects of your property plan into "chapters." The format should pretty much run as follows:

Cover Page
Statement of Purpose
Table of Contents
Executive Summary
Property Description
Market Analysis
Competitive Analysis
Marketing Plan
Management Plan
Budget

This is the logical organization of the information every plan should cover. I'll explain each of these chapter titles in greater detail, but first let me elaborate on the proper organization of your property plan.

Having a set of "questions to answer" about your property forces you to take an objective and critical look at your ideas. Putting it all down on paper allows you to change, erase and refine everything to the function in a manner of a smoothly well oiled machine. You'll be able to spot weakness and strengthen them before they develop into major problems. Overall, You'll be developing an operational manual for your property—a valuable tool which will keep your property on track.

Remember too, that statistics show the greatest causes of sponsorship failure is poor management and planning—without a plan to operate, no one can manage; and without direction in which to aim its efforts, no program can attain any real success.

Step 1.   Fabricate your Title Page

On the very first page, which is the title page, put down the name of your property with your business address underneath. Now skip a couple of lines, and write it all in capital letters: Property owner—followed by your name if you're the most senior member of your property. On the final plan, you might want to jazz it up maybe with some graphics. That's all you'll have on this page except the page number -1-. See the example on the next page.

Example (Cover Page)

A Sponsorship Opportunity Plan For :

Michigan Track Classic

February 1994
Ms. Julia Smith, President
Detroit, Michigan
(213) 987-2354

Step 2. Work-up your Table of Contents

Next comes your table of contents page. Don't really worry about this until you've got the entire plan completed and ready for final typing. It's a good idea though to list the subject (chapter titles) as seen in the example below, and then check off each one as you complete that part of you plan.

Example

TABLE OF CONTENTS

Executive Summary
Property Description
Market Analysis
Competitive Analysis
Marketing Plan
       Media Relations
       Property Outreach
       Publications
       Advertisement
       Public Relations
Sponsorship Plan
       Categories
       Packaging
       Sales
       Contracts
       Compliance
Management
       Administrative
       Marketing & Public Relations
       Operations
Budget

Step 3. Create your Executive Summary

The executive summary is the single most important element of a property plan. Having the power to make or break your plan, it must provide a concise, but clear picture of your program within a maximum of two pages. Designed to stimulate a busy reader's interest, the executive summary's job is to convince the reader to take the time to go over the rest of the plan in detail.

Among the points that you should cover in the executive summary are:

- The current status of your sponsorship program
- A description of your property
- Information about your target sponsors and your marketing strategy
- The key benefits inherent to your property that will enable it to achieve its objective
- Short and long term projections
- Amount of promotional consideration (cash, products or services) you're currently seeking

Condensing all this data to a two-page summary isn't easy. But, by staying focused on the key facts, you can do it. And remember that, even though the summary comes first in your business plan, *write it last*. That way you'll have the program in perspective and the information you need in hand.

Step 4.   State your Property Description

This section should begin with a statement of the organization's goals and objectives, defining what the organization does (or will do) and its purpose. This is the place to put background information about the founding of the organization, its legal structure, the nature of its industry, and the role the organization intends to play in it. You should also include information about the changes in the marketplace that will lead to an increased demand for what your organization has to offer. As you can imagine, sponsors are particularly attracted to growth markets.

Step 5.   Describe your Sponsorship Opportunity

Explain what your property sells or proposes to sell. Describe this in detail: for example your features, audiences, budget, available sponsorship packages and facts. Here its important to point out what separates you from your competitors' offerings and the benefits customers will derive from them.

Sponsorship Opportunity Profile

1. **Site.** Enter the city and state of the sponsorship opportunity.
2. **Name.** Please list the proper title of the opportunity for which you are seeking *sponsorship.*
3. **Category.** Reflects the type of sponsorship opportunity.
4. **Date.** State the specific date or date range of your sponsorship opportunity. If its organized over a number of days you can depict this with a Schedule Chart in an addendum.
5. **Primary Contact.** The name, title, company, address, telephone, fax and e-mail address of the person responsible for sponsorship at the property. This person must be in an authoritative position to commit benefits and accept promotional consideration on behalf of the property.
6. **Attendance.** Estimate the number and categories of consumers the sponsor would be reaching by entering into a partnership with your property to participate in your proposed marketing platform.
7. **Characteristics.** Enter the characteristics of the sponsorship opportunity: budget, charity or beneficiary.
8. **Special Features:** ticketed/free, program book, food/drink or media.
9. **Sponsors.** List the key partners (your perception) with the biggest brand value. If this is the first time your opportunity has been on the market, continually update this area as you secure major sponsors. This will demonstrate to other partners your opportunity is being purchased. For on-going sponsorship opportunities list your dominant sponsors from the previous year as you start the renewal and sales process.
10. **Sponsor Benefits and Description.** Provide a description and list major sponsor benefits of the sponsorship opportunity.

Please examine the example on the next page. Take this opportunity to develop your sponsorship opportunity profile.

EXAMPLE

Sample Sponsorship Opportunity Profile

Philadelphia, Pa

Fresh '99®
Community Celebration
April 29-May 3

Goldie Singleton, Sponsorship Director
Fresh'99® Community Celebration
P.O. Box 3252
Silverdale, WA 98383
Tel: (206) 692-1762 Fax: (206) 692- 3567

Attendance: 400,000   **Budget:** $1,750,000

Sponsorships are available for television broadcast, celebrity meet & greet, and entertainment stages. Official provider status, strategic partnerships and licensing are also available.

Sponsorships are customized to fulfill sponsor's objectives, and benefits may include signage, tickets, catered hospitality, sampling, tags in mass media, retail promotion, trade enhancement, exclusivity, and affiliation with the world's pre-eminent youth celebration.

Past & Present Sponsors: NIKE, Fox TV, General Mills, Coca-Cola, Kodak, Burger King, Nintendo of America Inc., Hallmark, Kindercare, Bristol-Myers, Nordstrom, Nabisco Foods, NBA & NFL Players Association, American Airlines, Walt Disney World and Duracell Batteries.

Fresh '99® United States largest youth festival occurs the third weekend in June. Celebrating its 8th televised year, Fresh '99® attracts over 8 million consumers. Fresh '99® offers three days of continuous entertainment featuring over 50 national entertainers, a celebrity meet & greet and a bite of United States.

Step 6.   Devise Market Strategy

The main reason for starting a sponsorship program is to sell sponsorships. That's where market strategy comes in. The primary objectives in this section of your property plan are to:

1. Define your target market by describing your potential customers and why they buy.
2. Estimate the total market size and determine what share of it you can realistically hope to obtain.
3. Develop a pricing structure that will ensure you maximum profitability.
4. Determine what combination of advertising and publicity to use to promote your property.
5. Outline a promotions strategy that will help you to reach your demographics in the most efficient way.

In spelling out these objectives, try to be as specific as you can, basing your market strategy on facts, rather than wishful thinking. Much of the information you will need to formulate your strategy will come from your budget information.

Step 7.   Competitive Analysis

Your competitive analysis should identify the key players in your industry and explain how your property can compete with them. Focusing on your strengths and advantages (as noted in your sponsorship opportunity description), you want to show how you can capitalize on them and gain market shares. Your purpose isn't to belittle the competition. Rather, it's to point out: (1) the customer's needs they are failing to meet, and (2) the limitations (such as being to large or inexperienced personnel) that keep them from doing what you can do.

One of the easiest way to gather information on your competition is by developing a series of survey questions and sending the questions in the form of a questionnaire out to each of them. Later on you might want to compile these answers into some form of directory or report.

Step 8.   Outline Management Data

In this section, you should outline the <u>job titles</u>, <u>duties</u>, <u>responsibilities</u> and <u>background resume</u> of the people involved in operating the property. You want to make it clear who does what (proposal preparation, sales, sponsor relations, management and so on) and who reports to whom. If you are currently an organization of one, describe the tasks you will be carrying out and estimate your futures sponsorship staff needs. To further illustrate how your program is set up, it's a good idea to include an organization chart in this section, along with position specifications.

It's important that you "paint" a strong picture of your top management and the people coming to work for you or investing in your sponsorship program. Individual tenacity, mature judgement under fire, and innovate problem solving have won more sponsors over than all the high prestige ratings and audience attendance put together.

Example

Position Title: Public Relations and Communications Manager

ROLE: **MAINTAINS PUBLIC AWARENESS OF PROPERTY ISSUES**
by:
planning and directing external and internal information programs.

ESSENTIAL TASKS:

1.   **SUPPORTS PROPERTY GOALS AND OBJECTIVES**
by:
developing external and internal information programs.

2.   **IDENTIFIES EXTERNAL AND INTERNAL INFORMATION NEEDS**
by:
researching trends; conducting surveys and analyzing responses; information requests.

3.   PLANS EXTERNAL AND INTERNAL INFORMATION PROGRAMS
by:
identifying audiences and information needs; determining specific media approaches.

4.   INFORMS PUBLIC AND STAFF
by:
developing and disseminating information, including fact sheets, news releases, newsletters, photographs, films, recordings, personal appearances, etc.; purchasing advertising space and time.

5.   RESPONDS TO MEDIA
by:
recommending information strategies to management; planning responses; providing information; arranging interviews and tours; editing copy; coaching responders.

6.   MAINTAINS RAPPORT WITH MEDIA REPRESENTATIVES
by:
arranging continuing contacts; resolving concerns.

7.   PROVIDES OPINION, OFFERS SUPPORT, AND GATHERS INFORMATION
by:
representing the organization at public, social, and business events.

8.   ACCOMPLISHES SPECIFIC INFORMATION OBJECTIVES
by:
designing and conducting special projects; establishing relationships with consultants and others.

9.   MAINTAIN HISTORICAL REFERENCE
by:
establishing and maintaining a filing and retrieval system.

10.   ACHIEVE FINANCIAL OBJECTIVES
by:
preparing an annual budget; scheduling expenditures; analyzing variances; initiating corrective action.

11. COMPLETES PUBLIC RELATIONS AND COMMUNICATIONS OPERATIONAL REQUIREMENTS
by:
scheduling and assigning employees; following up on the results.

MINI RESUME

Stephanie Coleman, VP of Public Relations & Communications

Stephanie Coleman is a public relations expert with over 15 years experience. She has a degree in Communications with post graduate studies in Marketing and Education. In 1989, Mrs. Coleman established her own public relations firm in Philadelphia. The firm, Third Eye Productions Inc. specializes in assisting mid-size corporations throughout the Philadelphia region to communicate effectively with the media through the placement of articles and the placement of advertisements. Ms. Coleman served as managing partner of this firm until joining the American Cancer Society.

Step 9. Describe your Operations Plan

This is the "nuts and bolts" section of your property plan - the place to describe how your sponsorship opportunity will actually be produced or delivered to your target audience. Information about facilities, equipment, and supplies all go in here. You should also explain what technologies, skills, and abilities are required to do each job.

Step 10. Prepare Budget Information

Last is the section of your property plan that we consider the "heart" of it, consisting of the financial data relevant to your opportunity. Suggested format:

- Cash
- Products
- Services

EXAMPLE

LINE ITEM	CASH	PRODUCTS	SERVICE	EXPENSE
Officials	$3,600			**$3,600**
Baseballs		$900		**$900**
Uniforms		$5,000		**$5,000**
Scorebooks		$60		**$60**
Venue Rental	$20,000			**$20,000**
Beverages		$1000		**$1,000**
Food		$2,000		**$2,000**
Trophies		$967		**$967**
Printing			$3,500	**$3,500**
Banners		$450		**$450**
Graphics			$2100	**$2,100**
Total	$23,600	$10,377	$5,600	$39,577

The most comprehensive and affordable, step-b-step sponsorship recruitment training program on the market!

Sponsorship Recruitment 101-102™
Self-Study Course

Module Six

SPONSOR ANALYSIS

A Crash Course for Identifying Active and Emerging Sponsor Categories

Anthony B. Miles
With Renee Crenshaw

6.0   Sponsor Analysis

While sponsor analysis might sound a bit dull, it is one of the most powerful competitive weapons available for the sponsorship seeker. It gives you insight into the desires and motives of your sponsorship prospects. When properly executed its like cheating - it gives you the answers to the "will they buy" quiz before you spend a lot of time and effort recruiting them.

Never stop asking sponsor's questions. Sponsors are the best source of information about the most effective way to offer your sponsorship opportunity. In addition to generating valuable insight on how to run your property, your sponsors will be delighted to give you their input.

3.2 Analysis Methodology

1. ***Define*** your target sponsors by category
2. ***Describe*** categories active role
3. ***Choose*** 6 brands in each category
4. ***Gather*** pre-recruitment intelligence
5. ***Analyze*** pre-recruitment intelligence

The task of finding the relevant information required may seem very daunting at first, but there is a great deal of information available from numerous sources. These sources may be broken down into three main areas: primary sources; secondary sources; and professional sources.

3.3 Research Sources
Primary sources of sponsor research
- Personal experience
- Questionnaires
- Personal interviews
- Staff
- Sponsors
- Suppliers

Secondary sources
- Conferences and seminars
- Libraries
- Industry sources (IEG, inc.)
- Trade journals
- Television programming
- Supermarkets

Professional Sources
- Consultants

Step 1. **Define** your Target Sponsors by Category

After you have completed an analysis of your property and budget, you will now posses the information to define your sponsors by category (see example below).

NBA ALL-STAR CELEBRATION™
Budget Summary

INCOME:

Awards Ceremonies		$2,203,000
Main Site	$1,878,000	
Satellite Site	$325,000	
Mayor's		$40,000
Pre-event dinner		$900,000
Post-event reception		$900,000
Benefit Concert		$525,000
Celebrity Basketball Challenge		
SmoothGear promo package		
Sponsorship		$10,700,000
Radio (52 @ $100,000)	$5,200,000	
Television	$2,000,000	
Top 4 partners	$2,000,000	
10 Support Partners	$1,500,000	
	Total Income	***$15,268,000***

Expenses:

Executive Cabinet		$549, 100
Marketing & Sales Group		$8,292,384
Sponsorship Marketing	$601,884	
Marketing & Endorsements	$7,200,500	
Media & Public Relations	$490,000	
Finance Group		$170,000
Properties Management Group		$2,293,000
Awards Ceremonies Production	$1,298,000	
Celebrity & Guest Services	$995,000	
	Total Expenses	***$11,134,484***

Executive Cabinet
General and Administrative

Salaries-Officers		$230,000
President, Marketing & Finance	$65,000	
President, Property Management & HRD	$65,000	
Chief Executive Officer	$100,000	
Salaries-Administrative		$70,000
Executive Assistant to President Marketing	$35,000	
Executive Assistant to President Mgt.	$35,000	
Office Expense		$8,400
Car Allowance		$24,000
Clothing Allowance		$36,000
Dues & Subscriptions		$5,000
Insurance-Medical		$10,800
Postage		$2,400
Rent(3 offices-executive center)		$40,500

390 square feet of office space
Executive furniture package
Access to conference room
All utilities
Janitorial services
Associated real estate taxes

Supplies	$4,800
Telephone	$7,200
Travel	$100,000

Airfare
Accommodations
Meals

Entertainment	$10,000

Total Executive General and Administrative   **$549,100**

Marketing & Sales Group
General and Administrative

Salaries		$129,000
Vice-President, Marketing	$46,000	
Vice-President, Event Marketing	$42,000	
Vice-President, Corp. Identity	$39,000	

Sponsorship Marketing Department
General and Administrative

Salaries-Support		$38,000
Director of Sponsorship Marketing	$38,000	
Bonuses		$100,000
Travel		$74,000
Entertainment		$20,000
Research		$11,384
Sponsordex (International Events Group)	$895	
IEG Sponsorship Report	$390	
Legal Guide to Sponsorship	$79	
Marketing		$4,500
Marketing Opportunities In Black Ent	$2,500	
IEG Event Marketing Conference	$2,000	
Outside Services-Public Relations Firm		$190,000
Identifying Partners	$10,000	
Appointment Acquisition	$20,000	
Sponsorship management & relations	$125,000	
Outside Services-Legal		$35,000
(Contract preparation)		
Total Sponsorship Marketing Budget		**$(601,884)**

Marketing & Endorsements Department
General and Administrative

Salaries-Support		$38,000
Director of Consumer Marketing		$38,000
Banners (5)		$2,500
Custom Portable Booth		$12,000
Mascot Costume (Dress Attire)		$6,000
Mascot Costume (Casual Attire)		$6,000
Consumer Marketing		$5,260,000
Radio (52 stations @ 100,000)	$5,200,000	
Invitations (Awards Ceremonies)	$60,000	
Event Marketing (SmoothGear)		$720,000
Sponsorship (13 Major Tournaments)	$200,000	
Radio (52 stations @ 10,000)	$520,000	
Travel-13 Major Festivals		$80,000
Travel-35 City Tour		$115,000
Travel-Endorsers		$100,000
Promotions(SmoothGear)		$661,000
Sweepstakes (Prizes)	$115,000	
Car or Sports Utility Vehicle		
Big Screen Television		
Trip to Music Awards		

Compact Disk	$30,000	
Studio Time		
Music Video	$100,000	
Merchandise Promo Package	$416,000	
CD Production		
T-shirt production		
Endorsements fee's (SmoothGear®)		$200,000
All-Star MVP's		
Michael Jordan		
Julius Erving		
Visible Movie Stars (3)		
High Profile Professional Athletes (3)		
Popular R & B Artist (3)		
Total Marketing & Endorsement Budget		**$7,200,500**

Media & Public Relations Department

Corporate Identity & Creative Solutions		$150,000
Promotional Compact Disk Design		
"Official Apparel" Catalog Design & Production		
Logo & Service Mark Development		
Commemorative Program		
General Program		
Outside Services-Public Relations Firm		$340,000
Media Relations	$135,000	
Press Kit Development		
Radio & TV Talk Show Acquisition		
Press Conference Organization		
Press Center Operations		
Magazine Interviews		
Business to Business Marketing	$10,000	
Interactive Solutions	$20,000	
Web Page for All-Star		
Web Page for SmoothGear®		
Celebrity Outreach	$25,000	
Co-host acquisition	$150,000	
Total Media & Public Relations Budget		**$490,000**

Finance Group
General and Administrative

Salaries		$90,000
Chief Financial Officer	$42,000	
Accounts Payable Coordinator	$23,000	
Accounts Receivable & Payroll Coord.	$25,000	
Supplies	$10,000	
Outside Services-Accounting		$70,000
Tax planning & preparation		
Human Resources Consulting		
Financial Accounting		

Total Finance Budget   ***$170,000***

Property Management Group
General and Administrative

Salaries-Management		$148,000
Production Director	$45,000	
All-Star Production Liaison	$38,000	
Special Events Production Coordinator	$28,000	
Celebrity & Guest Services Director	$37,000	
Salaries-Support	$30,000	
Celebrity & Guest Services Coordinator	$30,000	

All Star Production Department

Venues		$200,000
Equipment		$10,000
Security		$200,000
Credentials		$50,000
Entertainment		$172,000
Benefit Concert	$150,000	
Fashion Show	$20,000	
Celebrity Challenge	$2,000	
Awards Fabrication & Packaging		$100,000
Awards Fabrication	$70,000	
Awards Packaging (carrying case)	$30,000	
Outside Services-Ceremonies Production		$350,000
Producer Fee's		
Set Fabrication & Stage Set-up		
Backline Requirements		
Sound & Lights		
Outside Services-Concert Production	$12,000	
Backline (Sound & Lights)		

Outside Services-Fashion Show Production		$6,000
Outside Services-Insurance		$20,000
	Total Awards Production Budget	**$(1,298,000)**

Celebrity & Guest Services Department

Housing		$120,000
Deposit	$100,000	
Comp Rooms	$20,000	
Food		$625,000
Reception	$300,000	
Dinner	$300,000	
Breakfast	$15,000	
Comp Meals	$10,000	
Transportation		$220,000
Check-in		$30,000
	Total Celebrity & Guest Services Budget	**$(995,000)**

CATEGORY

Airline	Insurance: Property & Casualty
Automotive	Mail & Package Delivery Service
Audio, TV & Video Equipment	Media-Television Broadcast Rights
Bank	Media - Magazine/Newspaper
Beverage	National Travel Partner
Brokerage Firm	Packaged Goods
Car Rental Agency	Pharmaceutical
Carrying Case	Telecommunications: Long distance
Credit Card	Telecommunications: Cellular
Computer: Hardware & Software	Timepiece
Diversified Financials	Imaging
Document Processing	Insurance: Life & Health
General Retail	Logistics
Greeting Card	Petroleum
Hotel	

Step 2.   Describe Categories active Role

By looking at your targeted sponsors and what they do, it should be clear how the marketing partnership will work not only to support your property financially but to actually help you run your sponsorship opportunity.

Example: NBA All-Star Weekend

The following paragraphs describe the categories and how they will help the NBA All-Star Local Organizing Committee put on the most prestigious sporting events in the world.

Insurance: Health
This lead sponsor participates in all property events as well as provides health care insurance for NBA Properties and the Local Organizing Committee (LOC) members for the period they are preparing for the All-Star Celebration.

Automotive
The "Official Automotive" sponsor will be funneling more than 50 vehicles to the NBA Properties and LOC for transporting selected sponsors, athletes and other official personnel. Its message will focus on brand enhancement, showcase its technology and quality, and create excitement nationwide. Other parts of the sponsorship include a nationwide pre-event, on-site and post-event promotion with incentives to drive product sales. The promotion will have nonprofit overlay.

Telecommunications
The "Official Telecommunications" sponsor will contribute all the long-distance for the Celebration, providing expertise, equipment and service. Its most significant involvement will be the establishment and sponsorship of the 1-900 All-Star™ voting line.

Beverage
The "Official Beverage" sponsor will participate as the lead partner for the 35-City All-Star Hoop It Up following the celebration, which will bring the excitement to the enthusiasts unable to attend the Philadelphia festivities.

National Travel Partner
This "Official Travel Network" will be responsible annually for managing the Celebration travel. It will have an inventory of 5,000 rooms per night in each host city. It will also be responsible for hotel, airline and rental car reservations for celebrities, national sponsors, entertainers, public officials, professional athletes, media representatives,

Fortune 500 corporation's, business leaders, and other official personnel. *In addition, the "Official Travel Network" will assist in negotiating sponsorship agreement with a domestic airline, car rental agency, and mail delivery service.

Airlines

The "Official Airline" sponsor's mission is to fly the national guests to the celebration and get them home safely. Its sponsorship to the organizing committee is to provide air travel for athletes, sponsors, contest winners and other official designated personnel.

Car Rental

The "Official Car Rental" Sponsor will work with travel network to provide exclusive ground transportation for the celebration. Luxury, premium and full size cars will be issued based on the package level purchased. (i.e. Platinum, Gold, Silver or Bronze)

Mail Delivery Service

The "Official Mail Delivery Service" sponsor will support the All-Star Celebration by delivering official invitations to professional athletes, artists, government officials, celebrities, sponsors, media representatives and Fortune 500 executives. Then it will deliver approximately 10,000 invitations, 4,229 confirmations and over 1,000 credentials to media personnel. In addition, they will design a All-Star Celebration Commemorative Envelope for each host city. All package confirmations will be sent in these envelopes.

Cruise Lines

The "Official Cruise Line" sponsor will provide cruises for pre-event theme promotions tied to the nationwide voting campaign. In addition, this sponsor will have an active role by providing an official Caribbean music awards cruise as the finale of the annual celebration.

Brokerage

This partnership is designed to build brand value, develop/enhance community relations, entertain clients and solicit new business from high-net-worth individuals and corporate clients.

Banks

The bank partner will be providing celebration banking services for the LOC. This will also include a nonprofit overlay. Support programs will include a 25-cent donation from the sale of All-Star coins and $1 paid for each new qualified credit card applicant.

Audio, TV & Video Equipment

This sponsor will be the official supplier of broadcast equipment. This sponsor will design and install the broadcast center systems that will record this historical event.

Images gathered from the celebration will not only serve the general public (satellite site), but will also be fed on videotape for distribution. But the sponsor's single-most visible presence at the Awards will be the giant video screens used at the main site.

Document Processing

The document processing sponsor will be printing celebration results as they happen and creating an in-house publishing company for the media guide, and official and commemorative programs. In addition, this sponsor will provide the media center 10 copiers, 15 laser printers and 9 fax machines.

Logistics

The logistics sponsor will be responsible for providing ground transportation to transport other sponsors' equipment to the venues. Following the Awards Celebration this sponsor will also assist during the 35-City Hoop It Up Tour to transport all backline equipment.

Diversified Financials

This partnership is designed to build brand value, develop/enhance community relations, entertain clients and solicit new business from high-net-worth individuals and corporate clients.

Media-Radio

49 sports radio partners will provide promotional consideration leading up to, during and after the Celebration. This win-win relationship provides a forum to bring these stations together to strengthen their effectiveness, thus increasing the sports market share.

Media-Television Broadcasting

This Broadcasting sponsor will promote the Event through its independent affiliates as a prelude. Sponsor will exclusively broadcast the celebration nationwide. Also, the NBA Properties will seek support to televise the Tour.

Insurance: Life

This partnership will be designed to build brand recognition, provide community service and increase market share.

Insurance: Property & Casualty

This sponsorship category will provide comprehensive accident and liability coverage for LOC, NBA Properties and other entities.

Pharmaceuticals

This category sponsor's role will be designed purely to build brand exposure and possibly enter into a national charity tie-in.

Imaging

This sponsor will be addressing many challenges of the celebration. Most visibly, the imaging center will handle all the film exposed by media, photographers and the general public. Sponsor will also provide approximately 5,000 credentials for professional athletes, government officials, celebrities, sponsors, media representatives and Fortune 500 executives. The one-step identification will contain the image of the badge holder and coded with on access and identity information that is linked to a central data base. This sponsor's mission is to help people capture and preserve the special celebration moments, while helping to maintain a secure environment.

SUPPLIERS

Suppliers will form specific relationships based on the specific exactly what service or product they can provide. These supplies have narrow rights individually defined by their agreements.

Watch

This supplier will provide timepieces to the NBA Properties as well as to each game All-Star.

Awards

To consummate this partnership The NBA Properties will seek a crystal manufacturer to design and then produce the award annually.

Greeting Card

The greeting card sponsor will produce the All-star invitation. In addition the NBA Properties will license a NBA All-Star™ Commemorative musical greeting card for mother's day.

Now that you have created an active role for each sponsorship category you must now choose a minimum of six brands per category. List them in prioritized order bases on your preference. These are your sponsorship prospects. We have provided an example on the next page.

Step 3. **Choose** 6 Brands in each Category

TARGET LIST WORKSHEET (Sponsors)		
CATEGORY	PROSPECT	BRAND
Automotive	General Motors	
	Toyota	
	Landrover	
	Isuzu	
BEVERAGE	Coca-Cola	Coke
	Pepsi-Cola	Pepsi
		Mountain Dew
CAR RENTAL	Avis	
	Budget	
	National	
	Dollar	
	Hertz	
	Alamo	
Cruise Lines	Silversea	
	Princess	
	Holland America	
	Royal Caribbean	

TARGET LIST WORKSHEET (Sponsors)

CATEGORY	PROSPECT	BRAND
Telecommunications	Sprint	
	AT & T	
	MCI	
	GTE	
Audio, TV & Video	RCA	
	Sharp	
	Sony	
Airline	Northwest	
	US Air	
	American	
	Continental	
	United	

Step 4.   Sponsor Asset Inventory (SAI)

This worksheet is designed to help your property identify and accumulate and account for all the assets a sponsor will now be able to offer you in return for the marketable benefits you will offer them as your sponsor.

SPONSOR ASSET INVENTORY			
ASSETS	Carlson Travel	American Express Travel	Travel Agents Int'l
MEDIA		X	
Advertising Space			
Advertorial			
Balloons			
Blimps			
Billboards	X	X	X
Infomercials			
News coverage		X	
Promotional Spots			
Public Service Announcements (PSA's)			
Remnant Space			
Remotes			
Subway & Bus Advertising		X	X
Television Broadcasts	X	X	
Television Commercials			
Mini-Media			
Brochures	X	X	
Banners		X	
Signs		X	
Posters			
Newsletters	X		
Fliers			
Coupons			
Booklets			

SPONSOR ASSET INVENTORY (Cont.)			
ASSETS	Carlson Travel	American Express Travel	Travel Agents Int'l
Mini-Media (cont.)			
Circulars			
Door hangers	X		
Gift Certificates	X		
Stationary			
Shelf-takers	.		X
Bottle hangers			
Imprinted Grocery Bags			
Imprinted Register Receipts			
Targeted Media			
Customer Mailing Lists	X		
Postcards			
Inserts		X	
Catalogs		X	
Database Marketing			
Promotion			
Lotteries			
Sweepstakes	X		
Contests	X		
Music			
Jingles			
Packaging			
Frequent Buyer Programs	X		X
Point of Purchase (POP)			
Point of Sale (POS)			X
T-shirts		X	X
Premiums		X	

SPONSOR ASSET INVENTORY (Cont.)			
ASSETS	Carlson Travel	American Express Travel	Travel Agents Int'l
Promotion (cont.)			
Specialty Gifts		X	
Booths			
Entertainment/Hospitality			
Room Nights	X		
Parking Validations	X		
Food & Beverage Credits	X		
Meeting Space			
Distribution Channels			
Shelf Space			X
Ticket & Coupon Outlet	X		X
Non-Media			
Logo Usage		X	
Personality appearances			
Celebrities		X	
Endorsements			
Testimonials			
Market Research	X		
Cash	X	X	X
Graphic Design Services		X	
Commercial Printing			
Copywriting Services			

SPONSOR ASSET INVENTORY (Cont.)

ASSETS	Carlson Travel	American Express Travel	Travel Agents Int'l
Non-Media (cont.)			
Advertisers			
Creative & Video Production		X	
Advertising Sales Support			
Commercial Spot Production			
Voice Overs			

Step 5. **Gather** Pre-Recruitment Intelligence

"The probability of success in securing the sponsorship increases with the amount of knowledge we have before sponsor recruitment is started."

Successful sponsorship acquisition consists of having:
- The **right** marketing platform
- With the **right** assets
- Available at the **right** time
- For the **right** price

Your overall corporate marketing strategy should identify the categories which your property intends to concentrate (this is typically done in your Property Plan) and it identifies existing and prospective sponsors for whom these benefits are needed. In general, sponsors should have the following characteristics before any significant marketing efforts are expended:

- An identified need for the assets which your property has
- A desire to use sponsorship as a medium
- Ample funding

The overall marketing approach identifies the proper sponsor. The day-to-day marketing activities of your property consist of interfacing with existing and prospective customers to present your corporate image, identify sponsor needs, and align your resources to satisfy those needs. The single most important aspect of marketing is excellent performance on existing sponsor agreements. Every time that one of your employees interacts with a sponsor, there is a marketing aspect to that interaction. If we are building an image of competence, responsiveness, and caring for the sponsor in our daily activities, our sponsor will have a high level of trust for us, and all of the other aspects of marketing will be much easier.

Your probability of success in securing any specific sponsors depends upon an ongoing dialogue with your sponsors. First, if the sponsor's situation is right and you are sufficiently in his confidence, he may simply give you the sponsorship without asking other properties for their proposals. These "sole source" awards you the opportunity to bypass the often intense and costly effort of writing proposals, and they permit you to plan your work more effectively.

Most of the sponsor information should be readily available if the corporation publishes guidelines and/or an annual report. Some information such as what the sponsor will expect of the sponsored organization, may not be spelled out. Do your homework first; use an initial telephone conversation as an opportunity to confirm what you have learned through preliminary research (and to therefore show that you are on the ball!) and to fill in the gaps in information that was otherwise unavailable to you. If the decision maker is one individual, find out as much as you can through networking. This is a checklist of what you must know about every prospect in each category.

#1   Nature and History of Organization

- Purpose - why was it created
- When and under what circumstances
- What type of corporation is it

#2   Sponsorship Interest and Priorities

- Scope of support-property interests
- Exclusions -what won't they sponsor?
- Geographic area of interests; exclusions
- Scope of promotional consideration - cash, product or services
- Examples of properties they have sponsored, and proposals they have turned down

#3   Sponsorship Practices and Policies

- Smallest, largest and sponsor sponsorship size
- Total annual distributions (sponsorship)
- For how many years will they sponsor the same property?
- How many requests for sponsorship do they get on average in a year?

#4   Acquisition and Evaluation Process

- What types of properties do they sponsor? Are there any categories that are excluded from consideration?
- Steps properties must go through for decision
- Do they have published guidelines?
- Deadlines - when sponsorships must be submitted for consideration
- Preferred method of inquiry: phone, meeting, letter
- Review process: who reviews?

Step 6. Analyze Pre-Recruitment Intelligence

In all cases the sponsors will have specific needs or desires, which he/or she articulates. In most cases, the intelligence will not fully address all of these considerations, so a proposal written without closing the gap between the intelligence and the sponsor's needs (as viewed by reviewer) has greater chance of missing the mark. Contact reports, personnel who meet with the sponsors prior to recruitment, and experience gained on previous sponsors are all sources of pre-recruitment intelligence useful in planning the proposal.

"A proposal that matches the sponsor's needs has the greatest chance of winning."

Pre-recruitment intelligence is helpful in all aspects of proposal planning and strategy development, including:

1. Making the proposal/no-proposal decision - Is the sponsor biased toward another property or against your property?
2. Marketing approach - Has the sponsor indicated a preferred methodology for attacking the problem? Does he want a Cadillac job or something less?
3. Funding - How much money does the sponsor have to get the job done, and can you meet her needs for that amount?

For existing sponsor's, you can often gather this type of intelligence before sponsor recruitment. You can capitalize on your contacts within the sponsor's organization. For new sponsor's, prior marketing efforts may also provide key information. In some cases, however, we will have no meaningful information before sponsor recruitment is released. In these cases, consider the advantages of meeting the sponsor face-to-face to discuss her needs. This interaction will allow her to associate faces and personalities with names seen later in the proposal process and permit you to leave a favorable impression of your capabilities and experience. In this type of meeting, it is important to get the sponsor talking about his needs, and let him talk. The more he tells you the better your chances of writing a proposal that is responsive to his needs and desires. This association of names and faces tends to make the proposal evaluation more effective. If a face-to-face meeting is not cost-efficient, a conference call with the sponsor to discuss questions should be considered. On the next three pages are three examples of sponsor profiles for the Brokerage category.

Sponsor Profile™

Dean Witter Reynolds
Two World Trade Center
New York, NY 10048

Contact: Bob Sloss, SVP/Marketing Services Administrator

SPONSORSHIP CRITERIA

Sponsors mostly out of its 340 local offices. The six regional offices tie into properties that affect local offices. To be considered our marketing communications and proposals must meet the following criteria:

- access to affluent investors 40 to 60 years old.
- exposure and image fit.
- charitable overlay.

CURRENT OR PAST SPONSORSHIPS

- Santa Barbara Civic Light Opera
- Atlanta Symphony Orchestra
- Young Life Golf Tournament

APPROVAL STRUCTURE

Branch managers and regional managers approve deals for their respective areas.

Sponsor Profile™

Kidder, Peabody & Co.
10 Hanover Sq.
New York, NY 10005

Contact: Anthony Zehnder, Director, PR

SPONSORSHIP CRITERIA

The General Electric Co. subsidiary sponsor only out of its 51 branch offices. To be considered our marketing communications and proposals must meet the following criteria:

- provide visibility
- access to firms demographics generally aged 45 and older with profolios in the $300,000 to $400,000 range.
- opportunity to distribute premiums.
- provide client entertainment.
- charitable overlay and employee involvement is important.

CURRENT OR PAST SPONSORSHIPS

- Senior PGA Tour
- Southwestern Bell Classic
- Missouri Repertory Theater
- The Nelson-Atkins Museum of Art
- Philadelphia Welcome America
- Town Point Virginia Wine Festival
- Virginia Symphony

APPROVAL STRUCTURE

Managers in each office decides. Looking to coordinate sponsorships with other GE subsidiaries.

Sponsor Profile™

Legg Mason Wood Walker, Inc.
111 S. Calvert St.
P.O. Box 1476
Baltimore, MD 21203-1476

Contact: Bruce Genther, Acting Director of Marketing

SPONSORSHIP CRITERIA

The Legg Mason, Inc. subsidiary services individuals, typically aged 35 and older with annual salaries of $75,000-plus, as well as institutions, corporations and municipalities. The firm's 84 offices are scattered around the U.S. concentrated in the Baltimore/Washington DC area. Louisiana and North Carolina. Client assets in '93 totaled $16.7 billion, with company earnings of $36 million. Uses sponsorships, all out of corporate, as a vehicle to show they are involved in the communities and neighborhood they do business.

- access to firms demographics generally aged 35
- salaries $75,000-plus
- client entertainment with corporations, institutions, and municipalities.

CURRENT OR PAST SPONSORSHIPS

- IBM/ATP
- MLB's Baltimore Orioles
- Baltimore Festival of Arts

APPROVAL STRUCTURE

Genther screens proposals, subject to approval by Chairman of the Board. Sponsors mostly sports, but is interested in causes and the arts.

The most comprehensive and affordable, step-b-step sponsorship recruitment training program on the market!

Sponsorship Recruitment 101-102™

Self-Study Course

Module Seven

SPONSORSHIP PACKAGING

Creating Categories & Sponsorship Levels

Anthony B. Miles

With Renee Crenshaw

7.0   Create Sponsorship packages

The International Money Group model is a five step process that is used to create sponsorship packages. The five steps are shown below. These steps form a continuous loop.

Step 1.   Establish sponsorship levels
First you need to decide which will you use levels or categories. Then determine what levels or categories will you offer? Your decision on levels are based on your personal preference and the product or service categories are based on your budget line items.

Step 2.   Survey your assets
Take a look at all the possible tangible and intangible benefits you could offer to sponsors. This includes media, mini-media, targeted media, promotion, hospitality, distribution channels and non-media assets. Most of this you can pull form your property plan. After you have made a complete inventory of assets estimate the total value of each benefit.

Step 3.   Determine distribution of benefits
Based on the information gathered in step 1 allocate your benefits to your selected levels or categories.

Step 4.   Come to terms with media
After you have decided what media you will need to promote your sponsorship opportunity you then must go out and negotiate these assets with media properties.

Step 5.   Develop target list
This is the information you gathered in the sponsor analysis module.

We have provided a case study so that you can follow this methodology. After you have went through the process, sit down and create your packages.

EXAMPLE
Case Study

On Saturday, December 22, 1995 Portland, Oregon will get a slam dunk taste as Rasheed Wallace of the NBA Portland Trailblazers hosts the First Annual Rasheed Wallace Foundation Celebrity Sports Challenge. This exciting event will take place at the Rose Garden in downtown Portland.

The purpose of this nationally promoted event, organized by the Rasheed Wallace Foundation is to highlight the value of education and encourage Portland students to stay in school. Celebrities, athletes and entertainers from Los Angeles to New York will join Rasheed Wallace in promoting this worthy cause.

A partial list of celebrities who will be in attendance include box office favorite Danny Glover, pop star Mirah Carey, Laker Shaquille O'Niel, comedian Chris Rock, sports personality Dick Vitale and many more.

Other events planned in cooperation with the basketball game include a Star Gazing Reception and a press conference.

Step 1.   Establish sponsorship levels

Sponsorship Levels/Category Worksheet

Organization: <u>Rasheed Wallace Foundation</u>

Sponsorship Opportunity: <u>Celebrity Sports Challenge</u>

1. Which will you use?

☐ Levels

2. Which levels will you offer?

☐ Title   ☐ Presenting   ☐ Co-sponsor

3. Which categories will you offer?

None

Step 2.   Survey your assets

Organizational Asset Grid (OAG) Worksheet

Organization: <u>**Rasheed Wallace Foundation**</u>

Sponsorship Opportunity: <u>**Celebrity Sports Challenge**</u>

ASSETS	DESCRIPTION	VALUE
MEDIA		
Advertising Space	6 full page ads	$3,000
Advertorial		
Balloons		
Blimps		
Billboards	Two (2) 10'x20' boards (includes production)	$20,000
Infomercials		
News coverage		
Promotional Spots	Radio advertisements 150 :30sec spots	$45,000
Public Service Announcements (PSA's)		
Remnant Space		
Remotes		
Subway & Bus Advertising		
Television Broadcasts		
Television Commercials		
Mini-Media		
Brochures	4" x 11" (1,500)	$2,250
Banners		
Signs		
Posters	17"x 24" (900)	$500
Newsletters		
Fliers		
Coupons		
Booklets		
Circulars		

(OAG) Worksheet

ASSETS	DESCRIPTION	VALUE
MINI-MEDIA (Cont.)		
Door hangers		
Gift Certificates		
Stationary		
Shelf-takers		
Bottle hangers		
Imprinted Grocery Bags		
Imprinted Register Receipts		
Targeted Media		
Customer Mailing Lists	50,000 @ .10 per name	$5,000
Postcards		
Inserts		
Catalogs		
Database Marketing		
Promotion		
Lotteries		
Sweepstakes		
Contests		
Music		
Jingles		
Packaging		
Frequent Buyer Programs		
Point of Purchase (POP)		
Point of Sale (POS)		
T-Shirts	1000 @ $4.95	$4,950
Premiums		
Specialty Gifts		
Booths		

(OAG) Worksheet

ASSETS	DESCRIPTION	VALUE
Hospitality		
Room Nights	80 rooms (10 from 8 hotels)	$16,000
Parking Validations	10	$100
Food & Beverage Credits		
Meeting Space		
Distribution Channels		
Shelf Space		
Ticket & Coupon Outlet		
Non-Media		
Logo Usage		
Personality appearances		
Celebrities		
Endorsements		
Testimonials		
Market Research		
Graphic Design Services		
Commercial Printing		
Copywriting Services		
Advertisers		
Creative & Video Production	Video production	$1,000
Advertising Sales Support		
Commercial Spot Production		
Voice Overs		

Step 3.   Determine distribution of benefits

Title Sponsor

The title sponsorship is a fantastic marketing, public relations, and advertising opportunity. It is the most effective of our packages and receives the most visibility and exposure. It has unique coverage and targets multi-cultural markets, creating tremendous opportunities for product awareness.

Benefits

- Corporate name and/or identity will appear in the title of the event on all printed and electronic media and other printed materials, including, but not limited to:
  - Inclusion in media campaign, press releases
  - Newspaper advertisements; minimum of four inserts in top newspapers and publications
  - Radio advertisements average 100 spots
  - Taped interview opportunity with celebrity participants
  - Television advertisements (Public Service announcement campaign)
  - Souvenir program inclusion
  - All posters, flyers and billboards
- Press release on corporate sponsorship will be written and distributed to an exclusive list of local/national related media announcing corporate sponsorship at Title level.
- Inclusion in event advertisement within souvenir program booklet.
- Inclusion in extensive local/national media campaign, including but not limited to message specific interview opportunities both electronic and print.
- Introduction as a Title sponsor at initial press conference.
- Opportunity to co-host same-day Celebrity VIP Sponsorship Reception.
- Ten mentions in public address announcements throughout event.
- Unique in-arena and outside signage.
  - Prominent inclusion on all main event banners (2) 10 x 4
  - Individual banners (2) 3 x 8
  - Inclusion on prominent outside-arena signage, displayed at venue 13 x 5
  - Inclusion on billboard and bus advertisements
- Corporate signage on scoreboard.
- Cross promotional opportunities (inclusion in radio, television and event promotions). Title Sponsor can elect to work with other sponsors and retail outlets to develop related promotional programs.
- Exclusivity of product at venue:
  - One Vendor Booth (Space 8 x 10)
  - Display opportunities via unlimited sampling, pass-outs and/or couponing

- Right to use name of event and its affiliated celebrities in numerous approved promotional opportunities as associated with this event, such as: radio merchandising, sweepstakes, giveaways, and coupons.
- Ten invitations to all VIP functions, (i.e. press conference, pre-event celebrity and sponsor reception, celebrity after-party, post event).
- Exclusive arena suite (if available).
- Twenty tickets to event (limited additional tickets at discounted rate).
- First right of refusal to sponsor Title Sponsorship of future events.

Promotional Consideration: $25,000

Presenting Sponsor

The Presenting Sponsor is an extremely effective level of sponsorship, receiving significant visibility and exposure. This package includes the media campaign as well as exclusive association with participating event celebrities. The Presenting Sponsor will receive the following regional and national exposure and publicity opportunities:

Benefits

- Corporate name and/or logo as secondary part of title of event: "the Celebrity Sports Challenge" presented by (Your Name) on the following printed materials including all printed and electronic media, not limited to:
    - Inclusion in media campaign, and press releases.
    - newspaper advertisements; minimum of two inserts in top newspapers and publications.
    - Radio advertisements average 50 spots; Taped interviews w/celebrity participants as distributed to radio stations.
    - Mention in Television advertisements (Public Service Announcement)
    - Inclusion in souvenir program booklet.
    - Posters, flyers and billboards.
- Inclusion in event advertisement within souvenir program booklet.
- Inclusion in extensive local/national media campaign.
- Introduction as Presenting Sponsor at initial press conference.
- Opportunity to host same-day Celebrity VIP Sponsorship Reception – (in name only) Presentation to corporate representative.
- Mentions in public address announcements throughout the event.
- In-arena and outside signage: Your company logo placed throughout the arena on banners in strategic locations
    - Individual banners (2) 3 x 8
    - Inclusion on some billboard and bus advertisements
- Cross promotional opportunities such as inclusion in radio and television spin-off event promotions. Presenting Sponsor can elect to work with other sponsors and retail outlets to develop related promotional programs.
- Exclusivity of product at venue:
    - One Vendor Booth Space 8 x 10 (signage to be provided by sponsor)
    - Product/service displayed via unlimited sampling, pass-outs and/or couponing opportunities
- Right to use name of event and its affiliated celebrities in TBD promotional spin-off opportunities as associated with this event, such as: Radio merchandising, sweepstakes, giveaways, and coupons.
- Six invitations to all VIP functions sponsored by Presenting Sponsor.

Promotional Consideration: $15,000

Co-sponsor

The Co-sponsor is an effective and affordable means of involvement with this very highly profiled event. It is a simple package, allowing you to receive significant promotional exposure and publicity as well as economical flexibility.

Benefits

- Corporate name and/or logo on all radio and newspaper advertisements and on other printed materials (initial press release, posters, flyers, souvenir program cover).
- Corporate name mention in second half of radio advertisements, average 25 spots.
- Mention during taped interview (islands) with celebrity participants as distributed to radio stations.
- Newspaper advertisements: Minimum of two inserts in top newspapers and publications.
- Inclusion in event advertisement within souvenir program booklet.
- Event presented by (Your Name) as co-sponsor.
- Inclusion in extensive local media campaign.
- Limited mentions in public address announcement during actual event.
- In-arena and outside signage: Your company logo on banners in strategic locations throughout the arena.
    - Prominent inclusion on main event banners (3) 10 x 4
    - Individual In-arena banner (1) 3 x 8
    - Inclusion on billboard and bus advertisements
- Exclusivity of product and/or service at venue.
- Product or service will be displayed at every opportunity (sampling and couponing opportunities available).
- Three invitations to all VIP functions, (i.e. press conference, pre-event celebrity and sponsor reception, celebrity after-party, post event).
- Ten tickets to event.
- Right of refusal to sponsor/co-sponsor future events.

Promotional Consideration: $10,000

Step 4.   Come to terms with media

After you have completed the distribution of benefits you will now posses the information to come to terms with media partners.

Media

Media organizations continue to increase their level of involvement in the sponsorship industry. Partly in response to what their customers want and as a way to satisfy their own revenue objectives. Roles include; sponsor, broker, event owner and producer.

1. Daily and Weekly Newspapers/Magazines-Periodicals

The price per ton of newsprint has considerably restricted the amount of free space a newspaper or magazine doles out to worthwhile causes and events. It is becoming more common to see both philanthropic sources as well as commercial sources of space which are charged with being stand alone revenue centers.

Best Assets;

- Advertising space
- News coverage; editorial, features, local, entertainment, sports, business
- Advertorial; advertising department created stories and print promotions
- Zoned coverage (geographic, zip code)
- Graphic design services
- Commercial printing
- Advertising sales support
- Copy writing services
- Freelance referrals
- Volunteers
- Charitable tie-ins to their owned or sponsored events
- Internal publications
- Electronic services (phone, fax, on-line)
- Advertiser and community resources and contacts
- Market research
- Cash

Best contacts; Marketing/Promotion Director, Business Development manager, Advertising Director, Advertising Managers, Sales Representatives, Editors.

2. Network, Affiliate, Local and Cable Television

Television options are very diverse. The networks as well as network affiliates typically have limited inventories of air time. The independents have more available air time and tend to focus on syndicated content and more local issues. Cable television offers a number of diverse cable channels which target and attract specific viewers. Recognize the values of each and weigh your options appropriately.

Best Assets;

- Television air time: commercial advertising spots, PSA'S
- Charitable tie-ins to their owned or sponsored events
- Creative and video production resources
- News and special interest coverage
- Personalities
- Advertising sales support
- Freelance referrals
- Advertiser and community resources and contacts
- Internal publications
- Cable Television offers multiple cable channels, many with advertising options
- Market research
- Cash

Best Contacts; Public Affairs/Community Relations Director, Marketing Director, Promotions Manager, Corporate/Local Sales Managers, Sales Representatives, News Director, Programming Director

3. **Radio Stations**

    Stations continue to add sponsorship to their line up of marketing options to advertisers and even continue to create stand alone events which they can use to attract sponsors. The popularity of stations selling their sponsorship of events to other sponsors is also increasing and the partnerships can be a positive solution for all parties.

Best Assets;

-   Pre-produced or live liner commercial spots
-   Promotional spots or PSA'S
-   Charitable tie-ins to their owned or sponsored events
-   Copy writing services
-   Commercial spot production, including voice overs
-   Remotes. Subject to individual station policies
-   On-air personality appearances and endorsements
-   Listener/caller promotions on air
-   Internal and/or listener publications/newsletters
-   Mailing lists
-   Client tie-ins. Station may sell their partnership in your event to one of their clients
-   Advertiser and community resources and contacts
-   Advertising sales support
-   Duopoly opportunities. Multiple formats under one ownership
-   Market research
-   Cash

Best Contacts; Program Director, Promotion/Public Affairs Director, Sales Manager, Sales Representative, News Director.

Step 5.   Develop sponsor target list

TARGET LIST WORKSHEET (Sponsors)

LEVEL/CATEGORY	PROSPECT	BRAND
Title	ABC	
	NBC	
	BET	
	FOX	
	MTV	
	CBS	
Presenting	NIKE	
	REEBOK	
	ADIDAS	
	LOTTO	
	CONVERSE	
	FILA	
Co-sponsor	BURGER KING	
	COCA-COLA	
	KFC	
Sponsor	KEEBLER	
	SEARS	
	NESTLE USA	

The most comprehensive and affordable, step-b-step sponsorship recruitment training program on the market!

Sponsorship Recruitment 101-102™

Self-Study Course

Module Eight

SPONSOR RECRUITMENT

The Bible for Identifying Your Most Likely Sponsorship Prospects

Anthony B. Miles

With Renee Crenshaw

8.0 Sponsorship Recruitment

There are a number of preparatory steps that a property must take prior to sponsorship recruitment. No properties will have taken each of these preparatory steps prior to recruitment, but being prepared can facilitate the process and contribute directly to the overall success.

- **Organizational mission.** The organization should have a realistic, relevant mission statement that is accepted by the organization's and is the focus of its activities and program. If it does not, the recruitment presents an ideal opportunity to formulate one to revise an outdated statement.

- **Commitment.** Before the recruitment begins, the Board, administration, staff, and volunteers should be prepared to make a shared commitment to promote and support the recruitment — and eventually the program to the best of their abilities. General reluctance to do so probably does not bode well either for the recruitment or program.

- **Strategic Plan.** The Board and administration should have developed or updated a strategic plan that reflects sound administrative practices, including both short- and long-term objectives.

  This has to be a formal plan, keep in mind that sponsor's must be convinced that their investment in the sponsorship is capable of achieving commonly shared goals.

- **Sponsor Targets.** The targeted sponsor should be clearly defined.

- **Sponsor Recruitment Readiness.** The Board and administration should be prepared to follow through with the recruitment. We hope this module answers some of your questions about recruitment, and we wish you every success for the future of your organization.

Sponsor Recruitment Flow System™

Sponsor Recruitment is a prelude to proposal development. When conducted thoughtfully and professionally, this process will become the foundation upon which a successful sponsorship program is built.

In order to pursue multiple sponsors, it pays to follow a system that will maximize sponsor recruitment and ensure the correct processes are followed from your initial communications to the acceptance of the sponsorship proposal.

Following such a system will allow you to manage the production of increased proposals, thus increasing your odds of securing the right sponsors. Timely and appropriate communication with sponsors will also convey your organization's professionalism and seriousness with which you are pursuing their partnership.

Whether or not your marketing communications is accepted or rejected for consideration, and whether your next proposal is funded, remember to express your properties appreciation to the business or corporation at each step in the recruitment process. Those organizations are run by people like yourself who appreciate and remember acts of kindness. It's likely that you will one day be re-approaching the sponsoring organization, so it's important to maintain positive relations just as you would with any prospect. Sending a letter of appreciation following a rejection also allows you to ask for a critique of your proposal, pointing out both strengths and weaknesses.

Use the flow system as a way of increasing your efficiency and productivity. The system allows you to track contacts with multiple sponsors in each category and monitor activities at various points throughout the sponsorship-seeking process.

The more life you can bring to a proposal by making personal contact and the more you can distinguish your proposal from those with which you are competing, the greater your chances of achieving success.

Sponsor Category			
Recruitment Flow System	CBS	NBC	ABC
Letter of introduction & Sponsorship Opportunities Brochure	X	X	X
Call for appointment	X		
Acceptance/Rejection	Accept	Reject	Accept
Thank you to Rejection			
Add to Mailing List			
Date of Appointment	Sept 4th	N/A	Jan 19th
Thank you following appointment			
Research Sales Overlays			
Proposal Sent (with attachment)			
Proposal copy for site visit			
Thank you Letter following Appointment			
Date of Decision Making			
Rejected/Accepted			
Thank You Letter		X	
Amount Received			
Amount Requested	$25,000	$25,000	$25,000

As the sixth phase in the sponsorship acquisition campaign, the recruitment itself involves a number of sequential steps. The successful property takes these steps carefully, with the guidance of a sponsorship consultant. In fact, the recruitment process provides an opportunity to develop a strong, effective relationship between your property and sponsors.

Step 1.   Gather target lists

The acquisition team develops a target list of categories to be interviewed. Those selected are active or emerging brands whose demographics match yours. The number of interviews conducted is not of primary importance; rather it is the quality of those interviewed and the information they provide. For both large and small properties, the list typically contains 6 to 8 interviews per category.

Sample Target List (Beverage Category)

Mr. William H. Weintraub
SVP, Marketing & Sales
Coors Brewing
12th & Ford
Golden, CO 80401
Phone: (303) 279-6565

Mr. John Martini
Vice President, Marketing & Sales
Domaine Cardon
P.O. Box 2470
Yountville, CA 94599
Phone (707) 944-8844

Mr. Authur Shapiro
EVP Marketing
Joseph E. Seagram
375 Park Ave.
New York, NY 10152
Phone: (212) 572-7000

Mr. Steven Davis
Director of Marketing
Heineken USA Inc.
50 Main St.
White Plains, NY 10606
Phone: (914) 681-4100

Mr. Becky Madeira
Vice President, Public Affairs
Pepsi-Cola Co.
One Pepsi Way
Somers, New York 10589-2201
Phone: (914) 767-7761

Mr. Robert Davidson
SVP Marketing
Thomas Lipton
800 Sylvan Ave.
Englewood Cliffs, New Jersey, 07632
Phone: (201) 567-8000

Step 2.   Design marketing communications

After the list has been finalized, send each interviewee a cover letter with accompanying sponsorship brochure containing a brief description of your sponsorship opportunity, how this opportunity meets their priorities, and a request for an appointment to discuss a partnership. Each person is contacted to schedule an interview.

The most important aspect of any sponsorship recruitment effort is selling the sponsorship opportunity. Without sales, no program can exist for very long.

All sponsorship sales begins with marketing communications. To build sales, this must be seen and heard by potential sponsors, and cause them to react in some way. The credit for the program success, or the blame for the failure almost always reverts back to the cover letter and sponsorship opportunity brochure.

Generally the "copywriter" wants the sponsor to do one of the following:

a) Visit the property to see and judge the sponsorship opportunity for himself.

b) Entertain a meeting to identify the sponsor's priorities, or send correspondence which amounts to the same thing.

In order to elicit the desired action from the sponsor, all marketing communications are written to a simple "master formula", which is:

1) Attract the **"attention"** of your sponsor
2) **"Interest"** your sponsor in your property
3) Cause your sponsor to **"desire"** your property
4) Demand **"action"** from your sponsor

Never forget the basic rule of sponsorship copywriting the marketing communication must be written to stimulate sales; if it is not seen, it cannot be read; and if it does not grab the attention of the reader, it will not be seen!

Most successful sponsorship copywriters know these fundamentals backwards and forwards. Whether you know already or you're just being exposed to the knowledge and practice of these fundamentals will determine the extent of your success as a sponsorship copywriter.

SALES LETTER AND SPONSORSHIP OPPORTUNITY BROCHURE

Sales letter and Sponsorship Opportunity Brochure are the accepted marketing communications used by successful properties. This relatively inexpensive marketing communication gives the beginner an opportunity to market their sponsorship opportunity without losing their shirt. What is said in the sales letter and sponsorship opportunity brochure is the same as the proposal but in a condensed form.

To start learning how to write good marketing communications, collect ten sales letters and brochures that you think are pretty good. Analyze each of these: How did the writer attract your attention? Did it keep your interest? Are you stimulated to want to know more about this opportunity? Finally, what action must you take?

Rate each on a scale of one to ten, with ten being the best according to the formula I've given you. Now practice for an hour each day, writing the communications you have rated 8, 9 or 10. This will give you a feel for the fundamentals necessary in writing persuasive marketing copy.

It takes dedicated and regular practice, but you can do it. Simply remember and understand the basic formula - practice reading and writing good sales letters - and try to make the bad ones better. Practice, and keep at it, over and over, until the formula, the idea, and the feel of writing this kind of marketing communications become second nature to you. This is the only way to gain expertise in writing good marketing communications.

Sales Letter

Regardless of what kind of sponsorship opportunity you are trying to sell, you really can't do it without "talking" to the prospective sponsor. In attempting to sell by mail, the sales letter you send out is when and how you talk to your sponsor.

All winning sales letters "talk" to the sponsor by creating an image in the mind of the reader. They "set the scene" by appealing to a desire or need; and then flow smoothly into the "visionary" part of the pitch by briefly describing the sponsor's active role in the sponsorship opportunity. This is the "body" or guts of your sales letter.

Sales letters that pull the most sponsorship are almost always two pages. For big ticket properties, they'll run at least four pages - on a 11 x 17 inch sheet of paper folded in half. If the sales letter is only two pages in length, there's nothing wrong with running it on the front and back of one sheet of 8 _ x 11 paper. However, your sales letter should always be letterhead paper - your letterhead printed, and including your logo and business motto if you have one.

Regardless of the length of your sales letter, it should do one thing, and that's sell, sell hard! You should never be "wishy-washy" with your sales letter and expect to close the sale with your sponsorship opportunity brochure. You do actual selling and closing of that sale in the sales letter, any brochure you send along will only reinforce what you say in the sales letter. We have provided a sample cover letter on the next page.

(Sales Letter)

Memo

To:

From:	Jim Smith
Date:	March 26, 2004

Re: **"Official Imaging Sponsor"** for The Smooth Jazz Music Awardsô

The largest jazz celebration in the history of the United States has been created through The Smooth Jazz Music Network Inc., a Washington based corporation. This nationally televised celebration will annually recognize and reward the contributions of the entire jazz industry.

The Smooth Jazz Music Awardsô is a property that has a marketing platform with high-participatory demand that builds: <u>brand value</u>, <u>develops and enhances community relations</u>, <u>entertains clients</u> and <u>solicits new business</u> from high-net-worth individuals, corporate clients and general consumers. This property is estimated to reach **over 5 million consumers**, has nationwide charity tie-in and is supported by 49 Smooth Jazz Format Radio Stations. The Celebration consists of an Awards Ceremony (gala) with preliminary events (hosted annually by a different city) followed by a 35-City Concert Tour and a Cruise. Seattle has been selected as the inaugural site in 2001, followed by Los Angeles (2002) and Chicago (2003).

As **"Official Imaging Sponsor"** Polaroid will receive <u>significant visibility</u>, <u>category exclusivity</u>, <u>exclusive rights to sell film</u> which can be <u>co-oped with one hour photo finishing customers</u> on-site during all celebration events. Our key imaging objective during the celebration is to create an environment for photo-taking opportunities and to encourage people to purchase Polaroid film. We anticipate over 500,000 people participating in the Awards Ceremonies and the 35-City Concert Tour & Cruise. As you can see, our property provides an exceptional opportunity for Polaroid to gain market share from competitors **Eastman Kodak Co.** and **Fuji Photo Film U.S.A., Inc**.

I would like to schedule a meeting with you to discuss the specifics of this exciting, interactive partnership. I will call you this week to schedule an appointment. Thank you for considering this opportunity, I look forward to speaking and meeting with you this month. Please feel free to call me at *(360) 692-1762* if you have any questions.

Sponsorship Opportunity Brochure

Before prospective sponsors will give you cash, products or services, they want to know what you can do for them and how qualified you are to do it. At some point, you will need to make a presentation of your properties capabilities. A clear concise sponsorship opportunity brochure can be the means to get potential sponsors interested enough to give you a chance to meet.

Considerations when developing your brochure:
- create atmosphere
- adapt to sponsors needs
- be specific, brief but thorough
- acknowledge the needs of sponsor's
- be specific on what sponsor categories you what
- allow adequate lead time
- highlight your strengths
- document true figures
- don't oversell (let your demographics sell itself)
- recognize your weaknesses (play your strengths)
- be able to produce
- what's your track record

There are three main sections you should include in your brochure: company profile of your sponsorship opportunity, marketing opportunity & benefits and sponsorship opportunity analysis.

Company Profile of Sponsorship Opportunity

1. **Site.** Enter the city and state of the sponsorship opportunity

2. **Name.** Please list the proper title of the opportunity you are seeking *sponsorship.*

3. **Category.** Reflects the type of sponsorship opportunity

4. **Date.** State the specific date or date range of your sponsorship opportunity. If its organized over a number of days you can depict this with a schedule chart in an addendum.

5. **Primary Contact.** The name, title, company, address, telephone, fax and e-mail address of the person responsible for sponsorship at the property. This person must be in an authoritative position to commit benefits and accept promotional consideration on behalf of the property.

6. **Attendance.** Estimate the number and categories of consumers the sponsor would be reaching by entering into a partnership with your property to participate in your proposed marketing platform.

7. **Characteristics.** Enter the characteristics of the sponsorship opportunity: budget, charity or beneficiary.

8. **Special Features:** ticketed/free, program book, food/drink or media.

9. **Sponsors.** List the key partners (your perception) with the biggest brand value. If this is the first time your opportunity has been on the market, continually update this area as you secure major sponsors. This will demonstrate to other partners your opportunity is being purchased. For on-going sponsorship opportunities list your dominant sponsors from the previous year as you start the renewal and sales process.

10. **Sponsor Benefits and Description.** Provide a description and list major sponsor benefits of the sponsorship opportunity.

Marketing Opportunities & Benefits

1. What kind of marketing platform does your property provide?
2. Why sponsor your property?
3. What opportunities exist for marketers?
4. How do you help marketers leverage its sponsorship? What promotions have you created?
5. Key Benefits

Sponsorship Opportunity Analysis
1. Description
2. Audience Demographics
3. Programming
4. Hospitality Opportunities
5. Sponsorship Opportunities

Refer to the example on the next page. Your sponsorship opportunity brochure might not be this extensive but this provides a high level example to stretch your imagination.

SMOOTH JAZZ
MUSIC AWARDS
PROPERTIES

Marketing division of the Smooth Jazz Music Network, Inc.

What is Smooth Jazz?

What is Smooth Jazz?
A unique combination of smooth vocals and contemporary jazz instrumentals. America's escape from ordinary radio. New Adult Contemporary (NAC) music is rightly perceived as being hip, cool and creative by it's legion of fans. NAC aficionados can properly claim pride in artists such as the partial list below that all call NAC their home.

Kenny G	Najee	Spyro Gyra
SADE	Vanessa Williams	**Yanni**
John Tesh	Grover Washington Jr.	Patti Austin
Whitney Houston	Al Jarreau	Joe Sample
David Sanborn	**Tina Turner**	**Boyz II Men**
Eric Clapton	Chuck Mangione	Chieli Minucci
Michael Mcdonald	Alfonzo Blackwell	**Babyface**
Stevie Wonder	Pieces of A Dream	Brain McNight
Aaron Neville	Sting	Wyman Tisdale
Natalie Cole	Bob James	Paul Taylor
Lionel Richie	**Gloria Estefan**	Rick Braun
Anita Baker	Paul Hardcastle	**Rippingtons**
Patti Labelle	**Toni Braxton**	Doc Powell
Steely Dan	Richard Elliot	Harvey Mason
Herbie Hancock	Bobby Caldwell	Norman Brown
George Benson	Boney James	Dave Koz
Phil Collins	Count Basic	Pamela Williams
Luther Vandross	**Mariah Carey**	**Earth, Wind & Fire**
Billy Ocean	Michael Bolton	Jefferey Osborne

NAC listeners adore their artists and refer to them by their first names- "Boney", "Richard", "Luther", "Rick" just the way program and music directors do. Misconceptions about NAC run rampant everywhere-among ad agency buyers, in the consumer press, at competing stations in other formats and in parts of the record community.

Top 5 rankings 25-54 are a rule for many major market NAC stations. And in top markets, cumes in the 500,000 to 1 million range are now a reality. It's the fastest growing format in radio. About 70 Commercial FM Stations in cities large and small have made the switch, with more coming on board every month. NAC is expanding exponentially.

Smooth Jazz RADIO STATIONS

FORMAT: New Adult Contemporary (NAC). Unique music stations
               designed for adults seeking an "escape from ordinary radio".

MUSIC: Smooth Jazz is a unique blend of Smooth Vocals and
               Contemporary Jazz creating an uplifting, invigorating, soothing
               mood. Smooth Jazz has style, it's alluring, inspirational and sexy!

TARGET: Adults in their 20s, 30s, 40s and 50s.
               Core: Adults 35-54.

One of NAC's most striking and important qualitative characteristics is its multiethnic appeal: NAC's music is so universally appealing that it's colorblind. For many NAC stations, minority listeners comprise a significant - and particularly ardent - core group. While NAC, in many major markets, delivers African-American listeners in far greater proportion than they are represented in the population at large, NAC also flourishes in markets like Tampa, Portland, and Phoenix where minority listenership is relatively small.

Reach the best audience your money can buy. One of the most loyal and affluent audiences...

NAC delivers quality consumers
- Household income $75 to $100K
- College graduate/Advanced degree
- Professionals/Technical/Managers
- Business Owners
- Affluent Working Women
- Affluent African Americans
- Homeowners
- 3+ Air Trips annually
- Heavy Business Traveler
- Plan to buy PC/Software/Equipment
- Own Cellular Phone
- Brought or Sold Stock
- Frequent Users of Credit Cards
- Have CD/IRA/KEOGH
- 2+ Autos Owned

NAC listeners are sophisticated and culturally active
- Attend Opera/Symphony/Theater/Rock & Pop Music Concert
- Health Club 12+ times per year
- Wine consumed 3x per week

Smooth Jazz FORMAT RADIO STATIONS

KNIK 105.3	Alaska - Anchorage
KLBI 98.7	Alabama- Birmingham
KYFX 99.5	Arkansas- Little Rock
KYOT 95.5	Arizona- Phoenix
KEZL 96.7	California- Fresno
KSSJ 101.9	California- Sacramento
KTWV 94.7	California- Los Angeles
KSBR 88.5	California- Mission Viejo
KRVR 105.5	California- Modesto
KQBR 104.3	California- Sacramento
KXDC 101.7	California- Monterey
KIFM 98.1	California- San Diego
KBLX 102.9	California- San Francisco
KKSF 103.7	California- San Francisco
KHIH 95.7	Colorado- Denver
WJZW 105.9	District of Columbia
WFSJ 97.9	Florida- Jacksonville
WLVE 93.9	Florida- Miami
WLOQ 103.1	Florida- Orlando
WVAE 97.3	Georgia- Atlanta
KNWB 97.1	Hawaii- Hilo
KUCD 101.9	Hawaii- Honolulu
WNUA 95.5	Illinois- Chicago
WEZV 95.3	Indiana- West Lafayette
WJZZ 105.9	Michigan- Detroit
KCFE 105.7	Minnesota- Minneapolis
KMJZ 104.1	Minnesota- Minneapolis
KCIY 106.5	Missouri- Kansas City
WFAE 90.7	North Carolina- Charlotte
WNND 103.9	North Carolina- Raleigh
KRZN 101.3	New Mexico- Albuquerque
WHRL 103.1	New York- Albany
WSJZ 92.9	New York- Buffalo
WQCD 101.9	New York- New York
WGMC 90.1	New York- North Greece
WVAE 94.9	Ohio- Cincinnati
WNWV 107.3	Ohio- Cleveland
WJZE 97.3	Ohio- Toledo
KTNT 97.9	Oklahoma- Oklahoma City
KOAS 92.1	Oklahoma- Tulsa
KKJZ 106.7	Oregon- Portland
WJJZ 106.1	Pennsylvania- Philadelphia
WOTB 100.3	Rhode Island- Newport
KOAI 107.5	Texas- Dallas
KHYS 98.5	Texas- Houston
KCJZ 106.7	Texas- San Antonio
KBZN 97.9	Utah- Salt Lake City
WJCD 105.3	Virginia- Norfolk
KWJZ 98.9	Washington- Seattle

SMOOTH JAZZ
MUSIC NETWORK, INC. PROFILE

• Washington State Based Corporation

• Founded in early 1996 by Anthony B. Miles and Clinton Bush

• Purpose is to annually market and produce the Smooth Jazz Music Awards™

• Mission: To make Smooth Jazz Music Awards™ the preeminent music awards property that is respected by people throughout the world for its purpose, quality and goodwill and is found attractive by corporate and strategic partners for its excellence and tradition.

• The Smooth Jazz Music Awards™ will be along the lines of the:

  Grammy
  Country Music; and
  American Music awards

• Seattle has been selected as the inaugural awards ceremonies host city in April, 2001.

• New Orleans and Washington DC will serve as satellite sites.

• The Network 's key management team is composed of seven professionals:

  Anthony B. Miles, co-founder, Chairman, CEO and president of Smooth Jazz Music Awards™ properties
  Clinton Bush, co-founder & president contracts and site management division
  Anthony Flow, senior vice-president and production manager
  Marcus Miles, vice-president, licensing and strategic partnerships
  Jill Kenly, vice president, marketing & promotions
  Melanie Ferguson, vice-president, corporate identity and graphic communications
  Jamal Rivers, vice-president and merchandising manager

  Internal Support
  Accounting: Moss Adams LLP
  Counsel: Theresa Peeler esq., Arts & Entertainment law
  Public Relations: Conducting national search

  Key Contracts
  Television Broadcast Rights
  Smooth Jazz Format Radio Stations aggregated as a block of sponsors
  Host City Hospitality Event Planning Company

MARKETING OPPORTUNITIES AND BENEFITS

What kind of marketing platform does the Smooth Jazz Music Awards™ provide?
The Smooth Jazz Music Awards™ has a marketing platform with worldwide appeal that builds brand value, increases brand market share, develops and enhances community relations, entertains clients and solicits new business from jazz enthusiasts, high-net-worth individuals, celebrities, business, corporate clients and general consumers.

Why sponsor the Smooth Jazz Music Awards™?
The Smooth Jazz Music Awards™ is a spectacular event which will enable you to target by specific demographic segment (viewing, listening or live audiences) or as a whole to reach almost all demographic segments within the framework of one exciting and dynamic program. This high profile event will work for you by drawing your consumers into a unique environment. Within our event; your consumer base will have rewarding, exciting and memorable experiences.

What opportunities exist for marketers?
- Awards Broadcast Sponsors (ABS)
- Awards Ceremonies Partners (ACP)
- Licensing & Strategic Partners (L &SP)

How do you help marketers to leverage its national broadcast and awards ceremonies sponsorship? The Network has created the following official promotional vehicles:
- Smooth Jazz Music Awards™ World Wide Web Site
- Smooth Jazz Music Awards™ Merchandise Catalog Sweepstakes
- Smooth Jazz Music Awards™ 17-City Radio Station Concert Party Tour

Key Benefits:
- **Commitment:** An opportunity to work with an organization that is sponsor friendly
- **Advertising life span** of a particular product can extend through all our mediums
- **Access to affluent consumers:** thousands of high-net-worth individuals and corporate clients
- **large cumulative audiences:** The ability to reach millions of 35-to-54 year old professionals with graduate degrees, earning $75,000 to $100,000 annually
- **Pre-Awards** cross promotions with other participating sponsors
- **Product or service** placement and valuable third party endorsement opportunities
- **Guaranteed media**
- **Non-paid media** exposure and sponsorship exclusivity
- **Incremental sales**, product sampling and distribution of premiums
- **Rallying point** for your theme promotions.
- **Hospitality benefits with artists:** Premium tickets for distributors, dealers and retailers
- **Client entertainment** with high ticket demand

Awards Ceremonies

DESCRIPTION
An annual 3-hour live Smooth Jazz Music Awards™ telecast. The awards ceremonies provide a showcase where many of our nation's outstanding smooth jazz artist will be recognized and rewarded for their contributions. This year's awards host city will be beautiful <u>Seattle, Washington</u>.

AUDIENCE DEMOGRAPHICS
Viewing (Event Television): event will attract millions of consumers 25-54 and also capture the elusive teenage and younger adult audience.

Listening (Smooth Jazz Format Radio Stations): listeners 25-54 with college degrees, earning $75,000 to $100,000 annually, and are sophisticated and culturally active. That's the jackpot: baby boomers.

Live (Host City): 6,000 professional athletes, jazz artist, government officials, record label agents, celebrities, sponsors, media representatives, radio station and Fortune 500 executives. **Satellite site (Live Performance):** 16,000 celebrities, business leaders, jazz listeners and the general public. **Satellite site (Tribute Party):** 500 special guest.

PROGRAMMING
- Pre-Awards show (Broadcast live from host city)
- Awards presentations
- Live performances
- Documentary
- Tribute Party (Broadcast live on awards telecast from Washington D.C.)
- Satellite performance (Broadcast live on awards telecast from New Orleans Radio Station Concert Party)

HOSPITALITY OPPORTUNITIES WITH ARTISTS
- Pre-event Dinner & Fashion Show
- Post-event Reception & Ball
- Mayor's Breakfast

SPONSORSHIP OPPORTUNITIES
The Smooth Jazz Music Awards officials are selling a total of 29 sponsorship packages; 6 to be designated as national or ABS (Awards Broadcast Sponsors) and 23 to be designated as domestic, or ACP (Awards Ceremonies Partners).

By looking at the Smooth Jazz Music Awards™ targeted sponsors and what they do, it becomes clear how the marketing partnership will work not only to support this event financially, but actually help the Network and Host City put them on.

Airline
Automotive
Audio, TV & Video Equipment
Bank
Beverage
Brokerage Firm
Car Rental Agency
Carrying Case
Credit Card
Computer: Hardware & Software
Diversified Financials
Document Processing
General Retail
Greeting Card
Hotel

Insurance: Property & Casualty
Mail & Package Delivery Service
Media-Television Broadcast Rights
Media - Magazine/Newspaper
National Travel Partner
Packaged Goods
Pharmaceutical
Telecommunications: Long distance
Telecommunications: Cellular
Timepiece
Imaging
Insurance: Life & Health
Logistics
Petroleum

Step 3.   Interview sponsors

People who are inexperienced in securing sponsorships often see the entire process as totally impersonal. They view the sponsor profile as a black-and-white (and somewhat intimidating) document, behind which is an impressive sponsor machine that thought of everything. Part of gaining experience in this vital area is learning that the sponsor's organization is just another group of people - with weaknesses, and uncertainties, just like any other group. In fact, the sponsor's imperfections are often amplified by a large and cumbersome bureaucratic organization.

The process of interviewing is the process of listening and cultivating before you ask for cash, product or service. The interview should be conducted one-on-one in the sponsor's office for no more than one hour. Review the following questions to see which would be most beneficial or applicable to your organization and your knowledge of the sponsor. You may want to role play using these questions with other sponsorship team members.

1. Having reviewed last year's priorities and evaluation criteria, will there be any changes?
2. Which priorities are important to address in the proposal?
3. What is the expected size of sponsorships this year?
4. Is it permissible to submit more than proposal in a year?
5. Can you suggest other sponsors for which this sponsorship opportunity would be appropriate?
6. Do you review or critique proposals if they are submitted early?
7. What is the most common mistake or flaw in sponsorship proposals your organization receives?
8. Do you have any previously sponsored proposals we can read for format and style?
9. Do you use outside reviewers? Is it possible to speak to any of them regarding the things they look for sponsorship proposals?

Step 4.   Analyze data

After the interview is completed, the information is collated, summarized, and carefully assessed. This is when the acquisition becomes less of a science and more an art. When analyzing the results, please keep the following questions in-mind:

- Will the sponsorship opportunity help deliver business to the sponsor?

- Will the sponsor be able to achieve product/service marketing objectives with the sponsorship opportunities target audience(s)? (Is it the organizers job to market the opportunity; it is the sponsors job to market their product/service.)

- Does the proposed promotional consideration to sponsor the sponsorship opportunity accurately reflect the marketing benefit to be gained by the sponsor?

- Will media coverage of the sponsorship opportunity give the sponsor local, regional or national media exposure? And can it be developed or expanded by the sponsor?

- Does the sponsorship opportunity provide the sponsor with the opportunity to build client relationships?

- Is the sponsorship opportunity an appropriate fit with the sponsors image, and will it enhance that image?

- Does the sponsorship opportunity allow for appropriate input and approvals from the sponsor with regard to the sponsors product/service positioning?

If your proposal outlines how your sponsorship opportunity can market the sponsors product or service, therefore meeting their marketing objectives- not just provide them with a sponsor credit or logo - you will increase the likelihood of having your proposal accepted.

Learning From Marketing Communications That Was Rejected

I have historically secured about three out of four sponsors. One of the best ways to achieve this average is to learn from your losses so that you can improve your chances of success with the next prospect. An important aspect of successful marketing is listening to the sponsor, and there are few better opportunities to do this than during the de-briefing of an unsuccessful sponsorship recruitment.

"A good way to make sure we turn a no into a yes is to find out why we rejected."

The information gained during de-briefings will have value only if it is available to future acquisition teams for use in preparing their marketing communications. De-briefing information must be documented in a clear and useable fashion; it must be filed in an easily retrievable manner and it must be sought out and used consistently by the Sponsorship Acquisition Team if it is to have value.

Some sponsors welcome the opportunity to de-brief because they see it as an opportunity to obtain better future sponsorship opportunities. Some sponsors simply refuse to provide any information whatsoever. It is entirely proper and professional to request a de-briefing, either in person or over the phone, and the potential benefits can be substantial. Therefore, request for de-briefings are strongly encouraged; at worst, the sponsor will say no. At best, this can be a path to substantial future success.

A savvy marketer will be impressed by a mature professional who genuinely wants to learn how to improve future proposals. This is the proper attitude to assume on any de-briefing. A poor impression will result if we use it as a forum to complain. Remember, the de-briefing process can be an opportunity to make an impression on the sponsor that can help us to get future funding.

The most comprehensive and affordable, step-b-step sponsorship recruitment training program on the market!

Sponsorship Recruitment 101-102™

Self-Study Course

Module Nine

PROPOSAL DEVELOPMENT

A Systematic Approach To Preparing Customized Proposals

Anthony B. Miles

With Renee Crenshaw

9.0 Proposal Development

Talking about good news and bad news. The sponsor says, "Your sponsorship opportunity sounds great." That's good. Then the sponsor says, "Can you put together a comprehensive proposal for us that lays out the benefits, promotional consideration, your properties current and past sponsors, that sort of thing? Something I can take to my boss." That's the bad news.

"Your sitting on the key to millions"

Proposals are a painful reality of conducting any business. Anyone who sells a value-added solution, who positions themselves consultatively, who delivers a product or service that requires implementation, needs to write a persuasive customized proposal.

What is a sponsorship proposal?

In a nutshell, a sponsorship proposal is a presentation which answers a need stated by a request issued by a sponsorship prospect . The proposal responds to the priorities and objectives cited. The selected property is selected based on the evaluator's reading of the proposals—the quality, content, price and marketing platform.

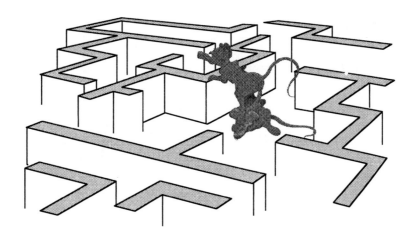

Therefore, a proposal, in this case, is a response to a request, and the request may be anything from a verbal request from an authorized corporate representative, to a one-page profile. Occasionally, you may submit an "unsolicited" proposal. That is, you are giving the sponsor a proposal which is not a response to a specific request. However, even "unsolicited" proposals have been discussed with the sponsor over the phone prior to submittal.

Since the proposal is key factor in determining sponsorships, there are some important factors to keep in mind when preparing it:

• Make a complete presentation. If you assume that the sponsor knows that you have worked with other corporations in their market sector successfully in the past, or have good sponsorship references, or have extensive promotional experience, you are probably making a mistake. The sponsorship proposal may have to "stand alone" as a total representation of your properties capabilities to people who do not know your organization. For example, the sponsor's brand management department may have sole responsibility for proposal evaluation.

- Focus on winning. Important factors include the following: a presentation slanted toward the sponsor's evaluation criteria; a good-looking proposal delivered in a timely fashion; a crisp writing style that stands out from the crowd; a well thought-out marketing approach; an impressive project team; sponsor references who sing your praises; and low cost relative to obvious value.

Although writing a sponsorship proposal is not easy, nor instinctively based on your previous methods, our 12-steps to developing effective sponsorship proposals will enable you to grow and be profitable.

3 Types of sponsorship proposals.

Solicited sponsorship proposals are submitted in response to request by a sponsor.

Unsolicited sponsorship proposals are submitted because of an suspected fit with your properties assets. The proposal is not competitive and is not a response to a request. An unsolicited sponsorship proposal must, first, convince the sponsor that your sponsorship opportunity address their priorities and objectives.

Sole-source sponsorship proposals are submitted for sponsorship renewals.

9.1   Making an Effective Proposal

Once your property has decided to respond to a the sponsor's request, you should focus the resources needed to secure the sponsorship within intelligent time and cost constraints. A "perfect" proposal would be one that secures the sponsorship with almost no effort (the "over-the-phone" business).

**"A proposal writing effort is like any other project;
it has technical, schedule and budget constraints."**

We use a rule of thumb that a sponsorship proposal should cost about one percent of the value of the expected promotional consideration. That would suggest that a sponsorship proposal for $100,000 should cost about $1,000 and that a proposal for $1 million should cost $10,000. Breaking this down for a "typical" proposal for $100,000 would permit a maximum of 50 total hours for all types of labor (e.g. professional, clerical, graphics and reproduction). For a million dollar sponsorship, the guidelines suggest that an effort ten times this large is acceptable.

No matter what the size of the sponsorship, the proposal will cost more than it should if it is not planned properly. A Sponsorship Acquisition Manager should immediately produce a rough proposal plan that shows what resources will be needed for what period of time. Obviously, if the decision is made start only a few days before the proposal is due, the Sponsorship Acquisition Manager will have little choice but to proceed in a crisis mode. This will result in a proposal being shipped out the door, in much worse shape than if we had more time, accompanied by a sigh of relief by the people who had to write, type, edit, print, collate, and fill out Federal Express forms. These things typically take longer than planned, and if the decision to start is held up for any reason, the Sponsorship Acquisition Manager is placed in an unnecessarily difficult situation.

Below shows the 11 steps in a typical sponsorship proposal effort. Subsequent sections of this text address proposal planning, production and follow-up in more detail.

1. Acquire the winning attitude
2. Develop property schedule
3. Analyze sponsor profile
4. Establish marketing strategy
5. Create outline, executive summaries and story boards
6. Draft proposal content
7. Determine proposal pricing
8. Evaluate proposal
9. Package & deliver document
10. Present proposal
11. Monitor decision process

The following list summarizes the key considerations in any sponsorship proposal effort:

- THE PURPOSE OF THE WHOLE PROPOSAL IS TO **SECURE THE SPONSOR**, not to produce a flashy proposal document.

- THE SPONSOR HAS A **NEED**. The more we know about the need, the more intelligently we can fulfill it.

- THE SPONSOR HAS A **LIMITED BUDGET**. The more we know about budgeting constraints, the better we will be in customizing a proposal that meets their budget.

- THE **SPONSOR** WILL PICK THE SUCCESSFUL PROPERTY. We need to learn as much as we can about how this will be done and tailor our proposal accordingly.

- **OTHER PROPERTIES WANT THE SPONSORSHIP**. We usually have to demonstrate that we can do it better with a higher return on investment. We need to MAXIMIZE YOUR STRENGTHS and COPE WITH YOUR WEAKNESSES.

- THE LONGER YOU HAVE **TO PLAN** THE PROPOSAL. THE GREATER YOUR CHANCES OF SUCCESS. This places a premium on up-front sponsor intelligence.

- SPONSORSHIP PROPOSALS **COST MONEY** (and elaborate proposals cost lots of money). Therefore, we should position ourselves wisely, and not be any more elaborate than necessary to secure the sponsorship.

- THE SPONSOR HAS TO **KNOW YOU**, or you won't get the request. Thus, we must be known by the sponsor to get a chance to present our sponsorship opportunity.

- COST IS **ALWAYS** A CONSIDERATION in selecting the sponsorship opportunity. In many cases it is the most important consideration. If possible, proposals should be submitted so that the sponsor has options to lower the total cost by reducing the benefits.

On a subject so complex, it is not possible to produce a "cook book." However, the 11-steps taught here suggest ways to increase your chance of success when submitting any sponsorship proposal.

Step 1.   Acquire The Winning Attitude

Often, a proposal will require capabilities from different departments to be combined to execute the benefits. These situations always have the potential to waste considerable time and money while the different departments "jockey" for position and debate such internal issues as which department will provide the Sponsorship Acquisition Manager and which cost center will get credit for the sponsorship sales. When any significant amount of time is spent debating issues such as these, it is usually an indication that time and money are being wasted, and the probability of securing the sponsorship is low.

"Since the sponsor will pick the successful property, it is vital to put forth the best possible proposal AS VIEWED BY THE SPONSOR".

The reason for this is that acquisition proposal teams flounder when they lose sight of the fact that it is the sponsor who must be satisfied, not our internal requirements. The sponsor has specified what he needs, and he is looking for the best property to deliver these benefits, the best price and within the required time. In many cases, the sponsor prefers to have certain people involved, and it is always best for us to offer these people. Winning acquisition teams never forget the sponsors orientation, and they place in proper perspective the internal organizational and other barriers to securing the sponsorship. There is ample time to make decisions on which department gets the sales credit, what people will ultimately be assigned, etc., after the sponsorship is secured. If you don't get the sponsor, (and a proposal that doesn't put forward the properties best capabilities is one sure-fire way to ensure that you won't), the opportunity to allocate sales will never come.

The way, then, to resolve all inter-department questions is to answer, Which approach is most likely to secure the sponsorship? and to answer this as the sponsor would.

The proper approach (and the winning attitude) is to find out as much as possible about what the sponsor wants and needs, then search throughout your property for the key benefits to deliver that, and to present them to the sponsor in a crisp, professional style that stands out from your competitors. No matter what department, division, or group ultimately receives the sales, your property will benefit from the resultant sales and profits - and that means that we all will profit. If your internal friction keeps you from winning, some other property will benefit from your short-sightedness.

Producing a proposal is a challenging task. There is seldom enough time to produce a top-quality product; there is usually other important work to be done at the same time; and there are often many different people from different groups whose efforts must be pulled together. On major proposals with significant "time crunches," much of the work is done late at night or on weekends; many meals are pizza delivered to the office.

Given these difficulties, proposal efforts can become "downers" - or efforts that tire people out and hurt their productivity on other important work. Good leaders can counter this attitude and capitalize on proposals to build teamwork and a sense of enthusiasm about their work. Figuring out how to beat your competitors, develop a unique marketing approach, or make your proposal look the best, or win over a tough sponsor - all these can become challenges which can make sponsorship proposals exciting and worthwhile.

Another important leadership approach is to encourage people not to remain emotionally involved with the sponsorship proposal once it's submitted. The vagaries of the marketplace are very powerful, and we often get turned down when we should win. No one likes to get turned down, but good leaders keep this from being discouraging for more than a few moments. The thing to do is to get up and keep pursuing the challenge of finding and securing more sponsors, and having fun at it.

To secure sponsors, it helps to have:

- The BEST
    - ™ People (and those the sponsor wants)
    - ™ Experience
    - ™ Marketing Approach
    - ™ Capabilities
    - ™ Reputation

• The BEST VALUE

Our chances of winning are hurt when we don't purpose the best we have to offer as viewed by the sponsor. With enthusiasm, a good leader can make even a difficult proposal into a worthwhile, challenging, learning, and fun experience.

Once the proposal is in, it's best to drop it emotionally and get on to other work (including more proposals). We often lose even when it's obvious we have everything going for us. Losing hurts less when we aren't hoping too hard for success.

• The BEST VALUE

Step 2.   Develop Proposal Schedule

It is the responsibility of the Property Manager to plan and schedule the acquisition process and control the associated costs. After the Acquisition Team has been selected and the marketing strategy is determined, the assignments for proposal development should be made.

**"No matter what the size of sponsorship proposal, the proposal
will cost more than it should if it is not planned properly".**

The Sponsorship Acquisition Manager should schedule key proposal dates including the following:

- Date due to sponsor
- Mailing date
- Reproduction date
- Final draft
- Team review (if required)
- Initial draft
- Status meetings
- Pricing approval

This schedule may be informally set or prepared as a formal schedule document (see Figure 9-1). In either case, it is important to factor in all key milestones and accurately estimate the time allowed for each. One approach to developing the schedule is to work backwards from the date of your sponsorship opportunity

ACTIVITIES	WEEKS			
	1	2	3	4
Proposal Meeting	x			
Write Rough Draft		x		
Type Rough Draft		x		
Initial Draft Complete		x		
Red Team Review Meeting			x	
Pricing Approval			x	
Final Approval			x	
Final Draft Complete				x
Mailing Date				x
Proposal Due				x

Figure 9-1. Sample Proposal Schedule

Step 3.   Analyze Sponsor Profile™

Sponsor's are just like any other group of people - there are those who are very experienced in using sponsorships and others who have very little idea of how this is done. Some are considerate of the properties needs and realize that if they can offer useful information, the property can provide better service. Others, for a variety of reasons, either resent or misunderstand the properties role and give misleading information. Accordingly, the sponsor analysis will vary in quality from those that give a thorough and complete picture of what is needed, to those that are confusing, incomplete, and poorly articulated. Each Sponsor Profile™ requires a careful review to develop a strategy.

When it is included, the MOST IMPORTANT SECTION in the Sponsor Profile™ is PRIORITIES AND EVALUATION CRITERIA. In this section, the sponsor tell how properties will be selected. THIS MUST BE THE BASIS FOR the MARKETING STRATEGY. Successful solicitors read the evaluation criteria FIRST, and then act accordingly. There is no sense in spending money on a proposal if the most important criterion identified by the sponsor is something we simply do not have - like commercial access in all 50 states.

The Sponsor Profile™ typically contains additional key information:

- Company name, address and phone number
- Contact person
- Evaluation priorities
- Demographics
- The brand company is interested in marketing
- Necessary tie-ins (i.e. retail or nonprofit overlay)
- Acceptable promotions
- Where qualifying groups should send proposals

Step 4. Establish Marketing Strategy

No two sponsorship categories have the same marketing approach. Hence, there is no way that any sponsorship proposal writing course can address the specific content of a proposal's marketing approach. However, there are some standard principles that apply when developing the marketing approach that can help provide a competitive advantage.

"The Marketing Approach must address the sponsor's and convey your understanding of the problem".

First, the marketing approach is the part of the proposal that requires the most creative thought. You must not only describe a technique for completing the work, but also must demonstrate an adequate understanding off the nature of the problem. Do not simply restate the their objectives and priorities. You must include some "meat" that describes in adequate detail how you intend to meet these objectives.

Winning themes associated with the approach should be carried through the entire discussion. These include key advantages to be gained by using your sponsorship opportunity such as:

1. An approach patterned after that used on a similar or identical sponsorships that was proved effective.

2. The availability of a unique medium to facilitate reaching your demographics.

3. The availability of a known expert in sponsorship to serve on the Acquisition Team.

4. An innovative approach that is more cost-effective and for which you have.

If pre-intelligence indicates an approach favored by the sponsor, our marketing approach should address that approach and use it if feasible. If pre-intelligence indicates that the sponsor would like to have certain people assigned to the sponsorship opportunity, their respective roles in carrying out the marketing approach should be indicated.

Finally, a good discussion of the marketing approach is organized in a manner consistent with the Sponsor Objectives and Evaluation Criteria. Terminology consistent with that of the intelligence should be used, and figures, tables and graphs should be used to demonstrate the approach.

When a short proposal lead time precludes development of a detailed marketing approach, consider presenting several work samples. The samples serve as an example of products that can be discussed only briefly in the body of the marketing approach. Samples could be included in bulk as a second volume to the proposal, conveying a higher degree of credibility

- Do not just simply restate the objectives or priorities.
- Describe in adequate detail how you intend to help the sponsor reach your demographics.
- Offer an innovative marketing approach.
- Carry winning themes throughout the discussion.
- Satisfy sponsor desires
- Organize according to the Sponsor Objectives and Evaluation Criteria
- Use figures, tables and graphs liberally.

Step 5.   Create Outline, Executive Summaries and "Story Boards"

The business classic, In Search of Excellence that the famous author John Steinbeck "...once said that the first step toward writing a novel is to write a clear one-page statement of purpose. If you can't get one page clear, it isn't likely that you'll get far with the novel." This principle is equally true for sponsorship proposals.

"You need tools to help you think before you write".

Once the decision to proceed with a proposal is made, prepare a detailed outline which complies with all the requirements of the Sponsor Profile™. In some cases, the Sponsor Profile™ dictate the outline in detail. Annotate the outline with a phrase or sentence tied to each topic which presents the overall theme of that section. The acquisition team should discuss and agree on the final annotated outline. Writing assignments can be made when more than one writer will be involved.

Experienced sponsorship proposal writers have found it useful to write a one-page Executive Summary at the outset of a proposal writing effort and to distribute this to all members of the acquisition team at the kick-off meeting. This one-page document should describe in crisp, clean language the major themes of the proposal, including the benefits to be delivered and the key reasons why your property can meet its marketing objectives. This document, when agreed upon by the acquisition team, can provide a clear focus for the team, ensure that the overall themes are picked up by the writers, and provide a consistency of approach that ties the whole proposal together, even if several writers are involved.

The classic use of an Executive Summary is to provide a very busy senior executive with a short, cogent, and complete picture of a document in a few short paragraphs. The use of an Executive Summary as part of a proposal writing effort can be very helpful, even if this document is not included in the final proposal. Whether or not the Executive Summary is in the final document depends on the requirements of the proposal (when we have a choice, it is usually preferable to include a well prepared Executive Summary).

A variation of the annotated outline that has proved useful in some proposal efforts is the use of a "story board." This technique was developed by the movie industry, and some companies have adapted it to the production of proposals and reports. The Sponsorship Acquisition Manager takes the annotated outline and prepares one page on each topic which includes the "headline: (or main thought) for that section, a sentence describing the section's overall theme (the thematic sentence), and any required graphics or illustrations. The proposal team then meets to review these sections. The story boards may be taped on the walls around a conference room, and the manager goes over the "story" of the proposal. While this approach may seem cumbersome or over-done, it has proved worthwhile on most proposals. It gets the proposals team to "talk through" the entire proposal in detail before beginning extensive writing efforts. This can provide an opportunity to produce a well-refined proposal and support efficient and consistent written efforts.

- BASIC OUTLINE
- ANNOTATED OUTLINE
- "STORY BOARD"
- EXECUTIVE SUMMARY

Figure 9-2. Tools to Help You "Think Before You Write"

Step 6. Draft proposal content

A proposal must communicate effectively. If your proposal is difficult to read, you will not convey your ideas to the sponsor, and you will reduce your chance of winning. The intent of this course is not to provide complete instructions in effective writing; however, these suggestions will enhance your sponsorship proposal:

1. Review the Guidelines in this Manual on Proposal Organization and Format.
2. Organize your thoughts.
3. Focus on the main topic or paragraph.
4. Structure paragraphs: Topic sentence, supporting sentences, transitional.
5. Avoid redundancy.
6. Eliminate needless words.
7. Avoid unnecessary commas.
8. Spell correctly.
9. Proofread all work (including corrections).
10. Avoid slang or jargon.
11. Allow charts and figures to be used without turning pages (where possible).
12. Try to get graphics facing text.
13. Use graphs and charts ("a picture is worth a thousand words").
14. Check for consistency with typing/style guides, particularly when several division are involved.

"A winning proposal must communicate the intended ideas to the sponsor."

As a minimum the sponsorship proposal should include:

® *a cover letter* written personally by the public relations or marketing manager, or with whom previous contact has been made, summarizing the main points of the proposal.

® *a cover sheet* outlining the full name of the property, name of company, date of proposal and the name of the event or activity.

® *an information page* outlining the facts about your sponsorship opportunity, the type of sponsorship being sought, the period of the sponsorship (include name, date, and venue), a schedule of activities, and the principal contact for the management of the sponsorship. Details about target market accessible to the sponsor, e.g. types of members, types of spectators, and dignitaries that will be involved.

® *an outline* of the sales promotions strategies and sponsor benefits, listing everything that will be provided to the sponsor with a value for each major asset category. This will later on be matched against the sponsorship figure requested.

® *the amount* of cash, product or service that is requested.

Proposal Template

COVER LETTER

The cover letter has been historically the weakest section of the proposal. Often it consists only of a few sentences with a brief description of the layout of the proposal. You should realize that the cover letter provides and opportunity to set the tone for the entire proposal, state our winning themes, and tell the sponsor why you are the best property for the partnership. The sponsor is usually most alert when he reads the cover letter and is most likely to retain the thoughts conveyed there.

"The objective of the Introduction is to convince the sponsor that he does not have to read the remainder of the proposal to know that your property is the best pick for the partnership".

When organizing the cover letter, focus on a presentation that highlights the Evaluation Criteria and emphasizes our strong points relative to each criterion. Don't restrict yourself to just the Evaluation Criteria; in many cases you might have a particular strength that sets us apart from the competition that is not specifically addressed in the Evaluation Criteria.

The cover letter (or at least its outline) should be one of the first sections written for the proposal. It should be concise, hard-hitting, and all inclusive of the key points to be made in the proposal. It should not exceed two pages in length. Make liberal use of boldface type, underline and other techniques to highlight key points. Remember your objective in writing the Introduction is to convince the sponsor that you are the best sponsorship opportunity to meet their needs without even reading the remainder of the proposal.

- Set the tone for the entire proposal.
- Organize around the Evaluation Criteria.
- State why sponsorship opportunity is the best, based on Evaluation Criteria.
- State winning themes and key points.
- Be concise and hard-hitting.
- Highlight key points with bold-face and underlining.
- **SELL THE SPONSOR ON YOUR PROPERTY.**

COVER SHEET

Proposal to Provide
Proposal Title

Prepared for the
Company Name
Site Located, State

For information concerning this sponsorship proposal, please contact:

Mr./Ms. Proposal Writer
Company Name
Street Address
City, State, Zip
(Phone Number)

EXCUTIVE SUMMARY

This should be a concise synopsis of the proposal which highlights the key selling points. It should definitely answer the question "Why your property?" You should avoid stating that your property is "uniquely qualified" unless it is an unassailable fact.

INFORMATION PAGE

As a prelude to the proposal itself it will be effective to outline briefly, yet powerfully, a synopsis of some key data. You should include: the type of sponsorship being sought, the period of the sponsorship (include name, date, and venue), a schedule activities, and the principal contact for the management of the sponsorship. Details about target market accessible to the sponsor, e.g. types of members, types of spectators, and dignitaries that will be involved.

Philadelphia, Pa
Fresh '99®
Community Celebration
April 29-May 3

Goldie Singleton, Sponsorship Director
Fresh'99® Community Celebration
P.O. Box 3252
Silverdale, WA 98383
Tel: (206) 692-1762 Fax: (206) 692-3567

Attendance: 400,000   **Budget:** $1,750,000

Sponsorships are available for television broadcast, celebrity meet & greet, and entertainment stages. Official provider status, strategic partnerships and licensing are also available.

Sponsorships are customized to fulfill sponsor's objectives, and benefits may include signage, tickets, catered hospitality, sampling, tags in mass media, retail promotion, trade enhancement, exclusivity, and affiliation with the world's pre-eminent youth celebration.

Past & Present Sponsors: NIKE, Fox TV, General Mills, Coca-Cola, Kodak, Burger King, Nintendo of America Inc., Hallmark, Kindercare, Bristol-Myers, Nordstrom, Nabisco Foods, NBA & NFL Players Association, American Airlines, Walt Disney World and Duracell Batteries.

Fresh '99® United States largest youth festival occurs the third weekend in June. Celebrating its 8th televised year, Fresh '99® attracts over 8 million consumers. Fresh '99® offers three days of continuous entertainment featuring over 50 national entertainers, a celebrity meet & greet and a bite of United States.

PROPOSAL

Even though there is no graphic or design styles to the proposal itself, we have seen very elaborate with fold out flaps and generic elements, to mid level 11 x 17 composition folded with a fly sheet in the center, to the very simple single letter. Whatever your preference is we recommend that you include the necessary elements, no matter how brief or elaborate.

We have provided you with this blueprint to organize your sponsorship data. In other words we will show you how to put together a winning proposal.

Sponsor Priorities and Marketing Objectives

Identify the priorities we gained from our research and interview of the prospective sponsor. Now we will demonstrate to the sponsor that your sponsorship opportunity has the marketing platform to meet its priorities.

Key Rights and Benefits

Here is were you offer specific tangible and intangible benefits to meet those marketing objectives that you stated in the preceding section of your proposal. Remember the idea is to provide key benefits and don't make a laundry list.

Promotional Consideration

This is where you ask for cash, products or services in exchange for the benefits you have provided the sponsor access to. Promotional consideration derived from sponsors is unrestricted. You can use it for the sponsorship opportunity being proposed or to relieve your general or departmental budgets. For example: the property plans to retain 2 of the 5 complimentary airline tickets provided below for general staff travel.

ADDENDUM

PERSONNEL QUALIFICATION AND MINI RESUMES

When writing proposals, keep in mind that what we are providing to the sponsor is the team of people needed to deliver the benefits. Too often, the Personnel Qualifications sections of the proposal and the accompanying mini resumes demonstrates a lack of appreciation of this fact.

**"If our proposal does not tell the sponsor why our Acquisition Team
is the best for the partnership, he will never know".**

The Acquisition Team Qualifications section of the proposal describes the properties organization and provide a organization diagram. This section should always include capsule summaries of the qualifications of key acquisition team members. The advantage of providing these capsule summaries is that they provide the opportunity to tell the client what you want him to know about each individual. Tailor this personnel qualification information to fit this proposal.

Capsule summaries of key acquisition personnel (e.g., Sponsorship Acquisition Manager, Sponsorship Acquisition Professional, Marketing Director) should be approximately one-half page in length. These summaries should stress the experience and qualifications of the individual relative to his or her function on the team. Shorter capsule summaries of other team members should emphasize for each individual the key facts that you want the sponsor to know.

Recall that mini-resumes should be submitted for typing early in the proposal production process since they represent part of the bulk typing that will need to be completed. "Standard" property resumes can significantly reduce typing requirements when these resumes fit the proposal being sold. Another reason for submitting resumes to typing early is that they can easily be left for last and go into the proposal without being tailored to fit THIS sponsor. This is a mistake and can easily blow the whole sponsorship deal. Read the resumes closely, and adapt as necessary. You cannot expect the sponsor to know the strong points about each individual on this proposal unless to tell him.

Finally, every project team has a set of collective strengths important to the success of sponsorship execution. That is why these individuals were selected for the team in the first place. In this section of the proposal, summarize these strengths and advantages for the sponsor. Usually this discussion will go in front part of the Personnel Qualifications section and referenced in the Introduction.

- Present Property Organization.
- Summarize key advantages of sponsorship acquisition team.
- Provide _ page capsule summaries of key personnel.
- Provide capsule summaries of project staff personnel.
- Use standard resume to fit each sponsor.

Figure 8-5. The Acquisition Team Qualifications Section

Example

West Sound Baseball Inc.

West Sound Baseball Inc. is composed of three executives from diverse backgrounds who have joined forces with the specific intent of annually producing an annual youth baseball classic. The network of professionals was established over 16 years ago and includes experts in the fields of Event Management and Corporate Sponsorship, Marketing & Promotions, Event Production, and Merchandising & Sales.

Wayne Bell, Co-founder

Wayne Bell, is one of the nations leading authorities on Event Management and Sponsorship with over 10 years experience. Wayne is managing partner in the law firm Bell & Associates and Vice-president of Competitive Edge Event Marketing. Wayne is nationally recognized veteran event producer. He also has a comprehensive knowledge and practical experience in marketing & promotions, entertainment & production, merchandising & sales, and public relations & communications. In addition, Wayne is considered one of the most innovative baseball sponsorship practitioners in the industry. Wayne actively as the Chief Executive Officer (CEO) of West Sound Baseball Inc.

Goldie Singleton, Co-founder

Goldie Singleton, is recognized as a marketing and sales genius with 17 years experience. He has established himself at an early age as a developer of creative marketing and promotions strategies. His marketing skills coupled with his extensive knowledge of consumer trends and promotions make Goldie one of the most resourceful leaders in an ever changing industry. Goldie is President & CEO of Goldie Singleton Entertainment a leading edge entertainment company which produces jazz, comedy, gospel and rhythm & blues concerts. His latest creation is two annual city-wide celebrations: "A Tribute To Miami" and "A Tribute to Denver". Goldie has served actively in several not-for-profit organizations and Goldie Singleton Entertainment has a lifetime commitment to philanthropy. He serves as Executive Vice -President and works directly with Wayne to lead West Sound Baseball Inc.

Gregory Jamal Rivers, Vice President of Merchandising

Gregory Jamal Rivers, who majored in Business Administration, has over fourteen years experience in the field of merchandising. His product lines have included both perishable and non-perishable items. Mr. Rivers has established a profitable business in the City of Detroit which employs several individuals. He has also marketed merchandise on a national basis and has established working relationships with wholesalers and manufacturers throughout the United States. His merchandise has been marketed in Atlanta during the 1996 Summer Olympics, in Las Vegas, and New York City.

REFERENCES AND PROPERY BACKGROUND MATERIAL

A record of past performance has traditionally been one of competing properties strongest selling points in getting sponsorship renewals with sponsors, and existing sponsors have often been our most effective salesmen in helping us to get new sponsors. In any proposal effort, it is therefore very important to capitalize on the positive aspects of sponsor references. Few factors carry as much weight with an evaluation as the knowledge that your company has done a great job with similar category on a similar project. And few promises, commitments, or fancy-looking proposals are not good enough to overcome a phone call from another sponsor who says that you have done a bad job and won't be used again.

**"The sponsorship reputation of your property and the individuals on
your acquisition team are key factors in winning sponsorships".**

The sponsor references section of a proposal can be the sole difference between winning and losing the sponsorship, so exercise care in completing this section. Not all sponsor recruitment have gone as well as we would have liked, and not all sponsor representatives will be as positive as we would like when providing references, even when we have produce results. It is therefore very important to use references that we are confident will help our efforts. It is both good business sense and common courtesy to check with these individuals before providing their names in a proposal. Reliance on a "boiler plate" list of references without checking that it is up-to-date can be counter-productive or even disastrous. In some cases, our most recent and highly appreciative sponsor's may be left off. In even worse cases, a strong anti-property person may be listed as a reference. Therefore, THE SPONSOR REFERENCES SECTION SHOULD BE REVIEWED WITH GREAT CARE. Similarly, our objective should be a standard of performance so high that any sponsor called at any time would give us the highest recommendation.

SPONSOR REFERENCES

Maryland State Fair has enjoyed good working and mutually beneficial relationships with our sponsors. The following is a list of sponsor references who are most familiar with our properties overall sponsorship execution. You are invited to contact any or all of these references.

Mr. John Kramer
VP, Marketing & Sales
Saab Cars USA Inc.
4405 -A Saab Dr.
Norcross, GA 30093
Phone: (404) 279-6582

Mr. Richard A. Hammill
SVP, Marketing
Home Depot Inc.
2727 Paces Ferry Rd.
Atlanta, GA 30339-4024
Phone: (404) 433-8211

Mr. Scott McHenry
Sr. Vice President, Marketing
Dial Corp.
15501 N. Dial Blvd.
Scottsdale, Arizona 85260
Phone (602) 754-3425

Mr. Tom Cardella
Vice President, Marketing
Labatt USA Inc.
23 Old King's Hwy. S.
Darien, Connecticut 06820
Phone: (203) 656-1876

Mr. David Samson
VP Corporate Communications
Levi Strauss
1155 Battery St.
San Francisco, CA 94111
Phone: (415) 544-1693

Mr. Mike Fidler
Director of Marketing
Pioneer Electronics
2265 E. 220th St.
Long Beach, CA 90810
Phone: (310) 816-0420

Mrs. Paige Perdersen
Director of Public Relations
Louis Vuitton
130 E. 59th
New York, NY 10022
Phone: (212) 572-9700

Mr. Charles R. Schwab
Chief Executive Officer
Charles Schwab Corp.
101 Montgomery St.
San Francisco, CA 94104
Phone: (415) 627-7000

Figure A-1. Sample Reference List

Proposal production efforts are intense because the time is short, and there are so many other things to do. It often seems expedient to take shortcuts on certain sections and to develop and use pre-prepared standard words or "boiler plate." These sections are particularly helpful in areas such as Property Background and History, Corporate Resources, Sponsor Lists, and other topics that lend themselves to generic discussions.

As time and cost saving devices, these tools are excellent, and their use is encouraged. However, the history of the Property is complete with examples where the wrong "boiler plate" was pulled out of the file at the last minute and thrown in without review, resulting in embarrassment (e.g., we sent a great list of Beverage-related benefits to the Automotive category or sent some glowing Television-oriented language to a potential bank sponsor). The message is clear - when throwing "boiler plate" into the proposal without reading every word and evaluating how it will affect our chances, we may be guaranteeing that we get rejected.

Here are some other items you should include: color or black & white photos of sponsorship in action, site maps, detailed customer demographic information and sponsor testimonials.

Step 7.   Determine proposal pricing

One of the trickiest aspects of sponsorship is pricing. Most properties do not calculate sponsorship cost and value. Without this knowledge, the property is likely to undervalue the sponsorship. While their is no one way to price this session will give you the confidence when calculating sponsorship value.

The strategy we use is qualitative and quantitative approach in our presentation to sponsors. This is a two step process:

1. First, calculate the value of the sponsorship tangible benefits. What tangible benefits will you will provide in return for the cash, products or service paid by the sponsor.

The value you assign will vary depending on local costs and conventions, such as local printing costs, advertising costs, etc. There a some other factors to keep in mind. In paid media for sponsorship opportunity, sponsor acknowledgment only represents about 10% of your guaranteed media buy. Say your media budget is $55,000, you charge the sponsor 10% of that cost, or $5,500.

SPONSORSHIP PRICING MATRIX

ASSETS	NUMBER	AMOUNT	CALCULATION	VALUE
MEDIA				
Advertising Space	700 col. inch.	$25,000	$25,000 x 10%	$2,500
Advertorial				
Balloons				
Blimps				
Billboards				
Infomercials				
News coverage				
Promotional Spots	100@ :30 sec with sponsor ID	$300 avg. CP:30	100 x $300 x 10%	$3,000
Public Service Announcements (PSA's)				
Remnant Space				
Remotes				
Subway & Bus Advertising				
Television Broadcasts				
Television Commercials				
				$5,500
Mini-Media				
Brochures	200,000	$0.005 per impression	200,000 x $0.005	$1,000
Banners	20	$0.0025 per impression	20 x 30,000 live audience x $0.0025 per impression	$1,500
Signs				
Posters				
Newsletters				
Fliers	50,000	$0.02 per impression	50,000 x $0.02	$1,000
Coupons				
Booklets	1 pg. in color	$15,000	1 x $15,000	$15,000
Circulars				
				$18,500

SPONSORSHIP PRICING MATRIX (Cont.)

ASSETS	NUMBER	AMOUNT	CALCULATION	VALUE
MINI-MEDIA (Cont.)				
Door hangers				
Gift Certificates				
Stationary				
Shelf-takers				
Bottle hangers				
Imprinted Grocery Bags				
Imprinted Register Receipts				
Targeted Media				
Customer Mailing Lists	30,000	$0.10 per name	$30,000 x $0.10	$3,000
Postcards				
Inserts				
Catalogs				
Database Marketing				
				$3,000
Promotion				
Lotteries				
Sweepstakes				
Contests				
Music				
Jingles				
Packaging				
Frequent Buyer Programs				
Point of Purchase (POP)				
Point of Sale (POS)				
T-shirts	27	$15.00	27 x $15.00	$405
Premiums				
Specialty Gifts				
Booths	2	$500 ea.	2 x $500	$1,000
Sampling	10,000	$0.15 per sample	10,000 x $0.15	$1,500
				$2905

SPONSORSHIP PRICING MATRIX (Cont.)

ASSETS	NUMBER	AMOUNT	CALCULATION	VALUE
Hospitality				
Room Nights	3	$189	3 x $189	$567
Parking Validations	27	$6.00	27 x $6.00	$162
Food & Beverage Credits				
Meeting Space				
Tickets	27	$50 ea.	27 x $50	$1,350
				$2079
Distribution Channels				
Shelf Space				
Ticket & Coupon Outlet				
Non-Media				
Logo Usage				
Personality appearances				
Celebrities				
Endorsements				
Testimonials				
Market Research				
Graphic Design Services				
Commercial Printing				
Copywriting Services				
Advertisers				
Creative & Video Production				
Advertising Sales Support				
Commercial Spot Production				
Voice Overs				
			Total Qualitative Value	**$31,984**

You have now established a concrete value of $31,984. Some of this will offset part of your sponsorship cost. (For example, the foregone revenue from the full-page ad in the program booklet.) Equally important, however, it proves that you have an understanding of your business and of the concrete value are providing. But there is author level of value-qualitative association-the value that rubs off on the sponsor by partnering with you. It is essential to estimate the value of qualitative association, too, before entertaining price negotiations.

To calculate your qualitative value, build a matrix listing the assets an association a sponsorship opportunity brings to the sponsor. The list might include the following:

- Awareness Level of the Sponsorship Opportunity
- Prestige of the Sponsorship Program
- Prestige of the Sponsorship Opportunity
- Desirability of the Audience to Sponsor
- Client Entertainment Opportunities
- Sponsorship Acquisition Expertise
- The loyalty of your Audience
- Length of Window of Opportunity
- Sponsorship Exclusivity
- Hospitality opportunities with celebrities

Once the list is has been determined, rate the value of those benefits on a scale of one to five (with five representing top value). We have provided figure 7-1 as an example. The average of the qualitative association assets is 3.8 and the value of the quantitative benefits provided the sponsor is $31,984. To estimate the total value of the sponsorship, its asking price, multiply the benefits by the average qualitative benefit rating to arrive at the total value of the sponsorship, e.g., $31,984 x 3.8 = $121,539.

QUALITATIVE BENEFIT RATING (QBR) SHEET

QUALITATIVE ASSET	ASSET RATING
1. Awareness Level of the Sponsorship Opportunity	5
2. Prestige of the Sponsorship Program	3
3. Prestige of the Sponsorship Opportunity	4
4. Desirability of the Audience to Sponsor	5
5. Client Entertainment Opportunities	2
6. Sponsorship Acquisition Expertise	5
7. The loyalty of your Audience	3
8. Length of Window of Opportunity	4
9. Sponsorship Exclusivity	3
10. Hospitality opportunities with celebrities	4
Total Rating Points	**38**
Total Points/by the # of rating categories = Average AVR for Qualitative Assets	**3.8**

Step 8.   Evaluate Proposal

The best way to understand how to prepare a successful proposal is to consider what evaluators have to go through to select a winner. First, all evaluators, whether an individual or a committee, must ultimately satisfy their supervisors that the review process was handled properly. The individual who received a verbal commitment over the phone must have a discretionary budget which is approved on some basis (usually annually), or he must obtain someone's concurrence that the partnership is needed and he has obtained a fair price. Later, they must be able to show the marketing platform performed well, and that a greater value was received for the money spent.

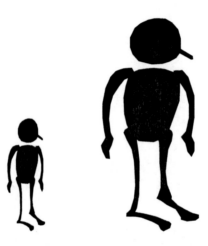

**"One or more people in the sponsor's organization will select
qualifying properties, based largely on the proposal".**

Imagine then, a case in which a committee is evaluating a dozen proposals. In many instances, separate Proposals are submitted, and they are evaluated separately. What will make the winner stand out from the crowd: Untold hours will be spent reading proposals from twelve different properties, most of whom are presumably competent to deliver the benefits. If you were reading twelve lengthy documents, all on the same subject, you would appreciate these features:

- A good appearance.
- Proper spelling and grammar.
- Crisp language.
- No more words or sections than necessary.
- Creative use graphics ("a picture is worth a thousand words").
- A unique approach to the problem.

- Good organization (i.e., keyed to the Evaluation Criteria).
- Ease in finding information (e.g., tabs).
- A structure that emphasizes what you're looking for (the Evaluation Criteria).
- Complete discussion of all required points.

These are important factors in preparing a good proposal.

Step 9.   Package & Deliver Document

Almost all properties Board members discourage elaborate proposals. Remember that a key objective in preparing your sponsorship proposal is to have it stand out from your competitors. Creative packaging of the sponsorship proposal can help achieve this objective as long as it is consistent with sponsors expectations and would not offend the proposal evaluation team.

"Proposal packaging should be consistent with the size of the sponsorship and the expectations of the sponsor".

In most cases standard proposal covers, paper, graphics, xeroxing and binding are adequate for proposals. When a really big sponsorship prospect comes along where more "flash" is desirable. The following options enhance the appearance of proposals:

1. Use of 19-hole hard-back binders with a unique cover design for the proposal.
2. Specially labeled dividers for proposal sections.
3. Specially designed title pages.
4. Better quality paper where the proposal is printed rather than xeroxed.
5. Artist-caliber sketches throughout the proposal.
6. Color photographs.

The costs of these enhancements vary widely. Graphics personnel or Corporate Communications can provide the Sponsorship Acquisition Manager with a wide range of options with associated cost and lead time requirements.

Step 10.   Present Proposal

Selling sponsorships consist of persuading a corporation that the property has the right combination of assets and experience to deliver. A very important vehicle that has occupied much of this module is the formal, written proposal. However, any interaction with the sponsor should be viewed as an opportunity to communicate, and thereby persuade.

"Effective presentations are sponsored-centered."

There are many of types interactions with sponsors that fall under the heading of "presentations" of "briefings" which are basically situations in which the property presents information to the sponsor in a reasonably structured format. In most situations, sponsorship presentations are made more effective by using some form of visual aid such as brochures, flip charts, overhead transparencies, or 35mm slides. Typical sponsorship presentation situations are:

*   one-on-one meetings.
*   a small property team presenting to one or two sponsors in an office.
*   one or more property staff presenting to several sponsor's staff in a conference room.
*   one or more property staff presenting to a group of sponsorship prospects.

Presentation situations pose several challenges. Generally, the purpose of the presentation is to communicate detailed information and concepts in a limited amount of time. Experience suggests that the more relaxed people feel and the more informal the atmosphere (with obvious limits), the more effective the presentation becomes. Relaxation and comfort come from confidence. Confidence come from knowing your property, being well organized, being fully prepared, and having solid supporting sponsorship material such as sponsorship opportunity brochures and visual aids. Figure 9-2 summarizes some of the key attributes of effective sponsorship presentations.

- Presentation is well timed.
- Sponsorship presentation material is well organized.

  Introduction
  - Properties top objectives and priorities
  - Meeting objectives
  Body
  - Sponsors corporate priorities
  - How your property meets the needs
  - Property strengths
  - Key benefits
  Conclusion
  - Next steps

- Presenter and audience is comfortable.
- Presentation is conversational.
- Sponsorship material is detailed and interesting.
- Sponsor feels free to interact.
- Visual aids are clear and easy to read.
- Presentation ends with clear understanding of the "next step".

Figure 9-2. Characteristics of Effective Sponsorship Presentations

Sponsorship sales is challenging. It demands the utmost of your creativity and innovative thinking. The more success you want the more dedicated you are to meeting your funding objectives, the more you will sell.

Here are some guidelines that will definitely improve your sponsorship sales, and quite naturally, your revenue. I like to call them the Strategic Sponsorship Commandments. Look them over; give some thought to each of them; and adapt those that you can to your own selling efforts.

1. Bring some visuals your sponsor can hold in his hands. In other words, get the sponsor "into the act". Let him feel it, and admire it.

2. Don't stand in front or alongside your sponsorship prospect. Instead, face him while you're pointing out the important advantages of your sponsorship opportunity. This will enable you to watch the facial expressions and determine whether or when you should go for the close. In handling you proposal, hold it by the top of the page, at the proper angle, so that your sponsorship prospect can read it as you're highlighting the important points. Regarding your proposal, don't release your hold on it, because you want to control the specific parts you the prospect to read.

3. With sponsor's who won't talk with you: When you can get no feedback to your presentation, you must dramatize your presentation to get them involved. Stop and ask questions such as, "Now, don't you agree that this proposal can help or would be of benefit to you?" After you have asked the question such as this, stop talking and wait for the prospect to answer. It's a proven fact that following such a question, the one who talks first will lose, so don't say anything until after the sponsorship prospect has given you some kind of answer. Wait him out!

4. Sponsor's who are themselves are sales people, and sponsor's who imagine they know a lot about selling sometimes present difficult obstacles, especially for the novice. But believe me, these prospects can be the easiest of all to sell. Simply give your sales presentation, and instead of trying for a close, toss out a challenge such as, "I don't know, Mr. Sponsor - after watching you reactions to what I've been showing and telling you about my sponsorship opportunity, I'm very doubtful how this opportunity can benefit you".

Then wait a few seconds, just looking a him and waiting him to say something. Then, start packing your proposal as if you are about to leave. In almost every instance, your "tough nut" will quickly ask you, Why? These people are generally so filled with their own importance, that they just have to prove you wrong. When you start on this tangent, they will sell themselves. The more skeptical you are relative to their ability to make your opportunity work to their benefit, the more they will demand that you sell it to them.

5. Remember that in sponsorship sales, time is money! Therefore, you must allocate only so much time to each sponsorship prospect. The prospect who asks you to call them back next week, or wants to ramble on about similar properties, prices of previous proposals, is costing you money. Learn to quickly get your prospects interested in, and wanting your sponsorship proposal, then systematically make your sales pitch through to the close, sign on the dotted line, and order you a check.

If you accept our statement there are no born sponsorship salesman, you can readily absorb the "commandments". Study them, as well as all the materials in this section. When you realize your first successes, you will truly know that "salesman" are MADE - not born".

Step 11.   Monitor Decision Process

Nothing is more disheartening than to expend a lot of effort producing a beautiful proposal and to have the proposal invalidated. This may be an omission of proper titles, required markings on the cover, not having pricing information, or any of a host of similar details that can be overlooked. Some of the silliest (and therefore the most painful) have to do with not getting the sponsorship proposal documents to the correct address (improper mailing labels) by the specified time (we didn't give our delivery vehicle enough time). Planning and attention to detail are the only way to avoid these problems. Check with the sponsor to make sure that he has received everything in the proper order by the proper time.

**"A sponsorship proposal is tracked until
the sponsorship is accepted or rejected."**

Once a proposal is received by the sponsor, it will undergo review and evaluation for some period of time before a decision is rendered. During the evaluation period, there is a fine line between showing an appropriate amount of interest in decision and becoming a nuisance. Sponsors who know us well will usually be fairly forthcoming with valuable information reasonably early in the process - "You're a little high (or out of the ballpark) on cost," or " Things look pretty good for you," or "No sweat, you've got it." Any data such as this is obviously helpful to a manager who is trying to plan the future workload for his staff.

Experience shows that the soundest policy is not to get emotionally involved until the official decision is announced. Some of your best contacts give out poor information (unintentionally, of course), and there's always a chance that someone "higher up" will override a decision that was headed our way. We often get rejected for sponsorships we should have won, and for all the wrong reasons. On the other hand, you will win more than your share, good luck.

10.2 PROPOSAL PREPARATION CHECKLIST

<u>Note:</u> This checklist is primarily used for use with sponsorship proposals. Please feel free to modify it so suit your own particular proposal requirements.

1. <u>Proposal</u>
☐ Prepare profile of sponsorship opportunity.
☐ Document sponsor objectives and priorities.
☐ Establish key rights and benefits.
☐ Determine promotional consideration.

2. <u>Packaging</u>
☐ Select cover design.
☐ Prepare cover.
☐ Determine how proposal will be packaged.

3. <u>Finishing Touches</u>
☐ Spell check all sections.
☐ Gather appendix.
☐ Prepare cover letter.

4. <u>Production</u>
☐ Determine where and by whom proposal will be reproduced.
☐ Check pages in each section for legibility.
☐ Check each copy to ensure no pages are missing.

5. Proposal Delivery/Logistics
☐ <u>Preparations for Delivery</u>
    ☐ Obtain packaging materials.
    ☐ Prepare label for proposal.
    ☐ Prepare receipt (for hand carrying).
☐ <u>Mailing</u>
    ☐ Check courier service schedules (#days required for delivery).
    ☐ Wrap proposal.
    ☐ Affix outside address label.
☐ Hand Carrying
    ☐ Make three copies of proposal.
    ☐ Make airline and hotel reservations.
    ☐ Wrap proposal and affix label.
    ☐ Affix outside address label.

The most comprehensive and affordable, step-b-step sponsorship recruitment training program on the market!

Sponsorship Recruitment 101-102™
Self-Study Course

Module Ten

SPONSORSHIP IN ACTION

The Blueprint For Maximizing Your Sponsors ROI

Anthony B. Miles

With Renee Crenshaw

10.0 Sponsorship In Action

Much of the work that was done in preparing a sponsorship proposal can contribute to the smooth and efficient execution of benefits. If the people who were involved in writing the sponsorship proposal are on the project, the project will probably get off an excellent start. If, on the other hand, the Sponsorship Acquisition Manager insists on disregarding the sponsorship proposal and decides to "reinvent the wheel," the future success of the project may be in jeopardy.

"The sponsorship proposal becomes a tool to help plan a sponsorship that was accepted."

While the proposal is important to formulating the sponsorship, the actual document governing the execution is the agreement. The proposal is often incorporated into the agreement by reference; however, agreement requirements sometimes differ markedly from the proposal or Sponsor Profile: the situation has changed; the sponsor has learned something new; or a similar reason.

Once contract negotiations are complete and there is clear understanding between the sponsor and property on the contract, the Sponsorship Acquisition Manager must start the internal process of assigning the people to the sponsor. Property Management assigns the Sponsorship Acquisition Manager and assists the Sponsorship Acquisition Manager in assigning the sponsor's staff. Whenever possible, the people who were identified in the proposals are assigned.

Step 1.   Prepare Sponsorship Agreement

In sponsorship as in any other business arrangements an agreement defines the relationship and provides clear definition of the who, what, when, where and why. In this agreement make sure you answer these questions:

1. **Sponsor's Official Status**
As only sponsor?
As only sponsor in category?
Right to approve other sponsors?
What about sponsorship of other sponsorship opportunities?

2. **Signage**
How many?
What is the size?
Who pays?
If sponsor, When will they be delivered?

3. **Acknowledgment**
On stationary?
In the name of sponsorship opportunity?
On program cover?
In program acknowledgment?
In all media?
In min-media only?
On promotional items (T-shirts, etc.)?

4. **Promotional Consideration**
How paid?
When paid?

5. **Renewals**
   Does the sponsor have the right to renew its sponsorship at the same terms and conditions?
   Does the sponsor has the first right of refusal for subsequent years?

No agreement between the property and sponsor - no matter how well defined and carefully thought-out can completely eliminate the possibility of misunderstandings, or even a stormy dissolution. After all the sponsorship agreement is only as solid as the undocumented trust between the two parties.

OFFICIAL TRAVEL NETWORK SPONSORSHIP AGREEMENT

THIS AGREEMENT (this "Agreement") is made and entered into as of the _____ day of _____, 1996, by and between Inc. ("Organizer"), More Learning Through Hope (MLTH) a corporation organized under the laws of the State of Virginia, and Travel Agents International® ("Official Travel Network"), a corporation organized under the laws of the State of Florida.

Recitals

WHEREAS. Organizer has the exclusive right to organize and conduct a youth celebration which is to be held during the month of April in Philadelphia (1998), Seattle (1999), Los Angeles (2000) and to be known as the Fresh '99 Celebration ("the event"); and

WHEREAS. Travel Agents International® has determined to provide cash, product and service support for the Event in exchange for certain promotional rights to be provided by Organizer;

NOW, THEREFORE, in consideration of the mutual agreements and promises contained herein, the parties hereto agree as follows:

1. **Official Travel Network Status.** Organizer grants to Travel Agents International® the exclusive right during the Term of this Agreement to use the Organizer's Trademarks as described herein in advertising and promoting TAI services as defined herein and refer to such services as the "Official Travel Network" of the Fresh '99.

2. **Advertising and Promotion.** (a) Subject to Organizer's rights of approval as described herein. Travel Agents International® shall have the right to use the Organizer's Trademarks in advertising and promotional activities only in connection with advertising its "Official Travel Network" status.

   (b) Organizer shall [use its best efforts to] provide the following rights to "Official Travel Network" during the Term of this Agreement:

   I. <u>On-Air Promotion</u>
   - Travel Agents International® will receive audio ID in a minimum of 1000 (:60sec) promotional announcements in our <u>4.8 million dollar radio campaign</u>.
   - The rights to purchase advertising spots on network, cable or other television broadcasts of the event licensed by the Organizer after the Top 5 sponsors has made its purchases;

II. Print

- Full page acknowledgment in the event program.
- Full page acknowledgment in the commemorative program.
- Logo ID on awards invitations.
- Rights to be named in all press releases issued by Organizer
- Rights to use the property logo in promoting Travel Agents International® services and refer to such as "Official Travel Network" of Fresh '99.

III. Hospitality

- Gold Package: Complimentary full service VIP packages for entertaining current and future clients (quantity to be determined).
- Complimentary special event tickets to use for promotions, giveaways and franchisees incentives.

IV. On-Site Presence

- 60 sec promotional announcement (by Roger E. Block) publicizing Travel Agents International® (380 franchisees) commitment to the More Learning Through Hope (MLTH) Network. This will be done following the tribute to the More Learning Through Hope (MLTH) during the celebration ceremonies narrated by a selected celebrity.
- Opportunity to provide Booth.
- Opportunity to provide signage at special events.

V. Sales Overlay

- Commission on Hotel Rooms (est. 10,000 room nights), rental cars and airfare per year for the next **THREE YEARS**.
- Ability to assist the Fresh '99 too sell-in the *airline, car rental, mail delivery* and *cruise line* of **YOUR** choice.
- Opportunity for celebrity endorsements.

VI. Value Added

- Charity Tie-in with the More Learning Through Hope (MLTH) Network.
- Data base marketing use.
- Category Exclusivity.
- First Right of Refusal for 2001-2003 partnership.

3. **Promotional Consideration.** In consideration of the full performance by Organizer of all of its obligations hereunder and all the rights granted hereunder to Sponsor, Sponsor shall pay Organizer the total sum of $ 300,000, payable as follows:

   $ 25,000   on or before November 1, 1996
   $ 25,000   on or before December 1, 1996
   $ 25,000   on or before January 1, 1996
   $ 25,000   on or before February 1, 1996
   $ 100,000   on or before May 30, 1998
   $ 100,000   on or before May 30, 1999

In addition Travel Agents International® agrees to provide the Organizer at its sole expense the following in-kind services:

- 20 Complimentary Airline tickets. On or before September 15, 1996.
- Nationwide Charity Tie-in agreement with the More Learning Through Hope (MLTH) Network.
- Monthly 1/2 page acknowledgment in **Travel News** (to promote charity tie-in, celebration, and sponsors.

4. **Option to Renew.** Organizer hereby grants to "Official Travel Network" the first right of refusal to renew its Official Sponsorship hereunder. Travel Agents International® shall exercise said option, if at all, by giving Organizer written notice thereof within 15 days after the 1999 Fresh . In the event that TAI does not exercise such option, the exclusivity described in Paragraph 5 shall nonetheless continue until the completion of the 2000 Fresh '99.

5. **Exclusivity.** Organizer represents and warrants that it will not authorize any seller of any product or service competitive to the Products [Services] or antithetical or incompatible with the Services to be an Official Sponsor or to be associated in any way with the Event.

6. **Trademarks.** (a) Travel Agents International® trademarks [service marks], label designs, product identifications, artwork and other symbols and devices associated with "Official Travel Network" Products [Services] (" Trademarks" [Service Marks"]) are and shall remain TAI property, and TAI shall take all steps reasonably necessary to protect such Trademarks [Service Marks] through U.S. federal registrations and foreign registrations as it deems desirable and through reasonable prosecution of infringements. Organizer is hereby authorized to use TAI Trademarks [Service Marks] in advertising and promoting the Event during the term of this Agreement, provided TAI shall have the right to approve all [the format of] such uses in writing in advance. [Organizer shall submit materials to TAI in writing and if company does not approve or reject such materials in writing within 5 business days after receipt thereof, then TAI shall be deemed to have approved such materials.] The rights to use TAI Trademarks [Service Marks] is nonexclusive, nonassignable and nontransferable. All uses by Organizer of TAI Trademarks shall inure solely to the benefit of "Official Travel Network".

Organizer shall not manufacture or sell, or license the manufacture and/or sale, of any promotional or other merchandise which bears Sponsor's Trademarks [Service Marks] without Sponsor's prior written consent.

(b) Organizer's trademarks [service marks], designs, artwork and other symbols and devices associated with the Event ("Organizer's Trademarks") [(Organizer's Service Marks")] are and shall remain Organizer's property, and Organizer shall take all steps reasonably necessary to protect such Trademarks [Service Marks] through U.S.

federal registrations and foreign registrations as it deems desirable and through reasonable prosecution of infringements. Travel Agent International® is hereby authorized to use Organizer's Trademarks [Service Marks] in advertising and promoting the Services during the term of this Agreement, provided Organizer shall have the right to approve all [the format of] such uses in writing in advance. ["Official Travel Network" shall submit materials to Organizer in writing and if Organizer does not approve or reject such materials in writing within 5 business days after receipt thereof, then Organizer shall be deemed to have approved such materials.] The rights to use Organizer's Trademarks [Service Marks] is nonexclusive, nonassignable and nontransferable. All uses by TAI of Organizer's Trademarks shall inure solely to the benefit of the Organizer.

Travel Agents International shall not manufacture or sell, or license the manufacture and/or sale, of any promotional or other merchandise which bears Organizer's Trademarks [Service Marks] without Organizer's prior written consent.

7. **Commission.** In consideration for assisting More Learning Through Network in securing additional partners the Network has authorized the following commission guidelines to Travel Agents International which will be independent of its sponsorship:

    Finder's fee: Five (5) percent of the total sponsorship amount will be paid to Travel Agents International for the introduction of Competitive Edge to one of its accounts or vendors but does little work to finalize the contract. "Introduction" means the Travel Agents International actually secures an appointment with the potential sponsor for Competitive Edge. The appointment must be someone who is in a decision-making position with the potential sponsor. The "finder" must be present for the initial meeting between Competitive Edge and a potential sponsor.

    Commission: If Travel Agents International introduces Competitive Edge to a potential sponsor and follows through and is a principal part of the negotiation with that sponsor up to the time a sponsorship agreement is finally signed, then Travel Agents International is entitled to 10% commission of the first year of the contract.

    When Payable: Commission fee's will be payable only for cash sponsorships and within 7 days after fee has been received by Competitive Edge. There will be no fee's for in-kind payments by sponsors.

8. Warranties. (a) **Organizer represents and warrants that:**

(i) it has the full right and legal authority to enter into and fully perform this Agreement in accordance with its terms without violating the right of any other person;
(ii) Organizer's Trademarks [Service Marks] do not infringe the trademarks or trade names or other rights of any other person;

(iii) it has all government licenses, permits or other authorizations necessary to conduct the Event as contemplated under this Agreement.

(iv) it will comply with all applicable laws, regulations and ordinances pertaining to the promotion and conduct of the Event.

(b) **Sponsor represents and warrants that:**

(i) it has the full right and legal authority to enter into and fully perform this Agreement in accordance with its terms without violating the right of any other person;

(ii) Sponsor's Trademarks [Service Marks] do not infringe the trademarks or trade names or other rights of any other person;

(iii) it has all government licenses, permits or other authorizations necessary to conduct the Event as contemplated under this Agreement.

9. Indemnity. Each party will indemnify, defend and hold harmless the other, its parent, subsidiary and affiliated corporations and their respective directors, officers, employees, agents, successors and assigns, from and against any and all claims, damages, liabilities, losses, government proceedings and costs and expenses, including reasonable attorneys' fees and costs of suit, arising out of any alleged or actual breach of this Agreement or the inaccuracy of any warranty or representation made by it or any act or omission by it or any act of omission by it in the performance of this Agreement or the purposes hereof.

10. Insurance. Each party hereunder shall obtain and maintain at its own expense, during the term of this Agreement and for a period of 1 year following the Event, a Comprehensive General Liability Policy written by a United States insurance company in the face amount of $1,000,000 each occurrence/$3,000,000 aggregate, which policy shall (i) specifically cover such party's incidental contractual obligations; (ii) provide standard product liability protection and (iii) list the other as a named insured. Such insurance shall be in a form reasonably acceptable to counsel for the other and shall require the insurer to give the other at least 30 days' prior written notice of any modification or cancellation. Each party shall provide the other with such evidence of coverage as may be reasonably acceptable to the other within 30 days following the execution of this Agreement.

11. Term and Termination. This Agreement shall become effective on the date first above written and shall expire on May 30, 2000, unless terminated earlier or renewed pursuant to the terms hereof (the "Term").

12. Cancellation and Preemption. In the event that the Event does not take place, in whole or in part, due to any Act of God or force majeure, including without limitation, weather, fire, flood, strike, labor dispute or similar cause beyond the control of both parties, then sponsor shall be entitled to an immediate refund of the Sponsorship Fee [or a pro rata portion thereof if the Event took place only in part]. Organizer will provide adequate rain, cancellation and preemption insurance to cover its obligations hereunder.

13. Miscellany. (1) *Confidentiality.* The parties hereto agree to maintain in confidence the terms and conditions of this Agreement except to the extent that a proposed disclosure of any specific terms or conditions hereof by either party is authorized in advance by the other party.

(2) *Notices.* All notices required or permitted to be made under this Agreement shall be in writing and shall be deemed to have been duly given when delivered or sent by prepaid certified or registered mail or telex:

> If to Sponsor, to: P.O. Box 42008, St. Petersburg, Florida 33742-4008
> If to Organizer, to: P.O. Box 3129, Alexandia, Virginia 98383

or such other address as either party may designate in writing to the other party for this purpose.

(3) *Non-Assignment.* Neither party shall assign this Agreement without prior written approval of the other party, except that Sponsor may assign this Agreement to any entity which acquires substantially all of its assets.

(4) *Complete Agreement.* This Agreement represents the entire agreement between the parties and supersedes all other agreements, if any, express or implied, whether written or oral. Organizer has made and makes no representations of any kind except those specifically set forth herein.

(5) *Binding Agreement.* This Agreement shall be binding upon the parties, their successors and assigns.

IN WITNESS WHEREOF, the parties have executed this Agreement on the date first above written.

Travel Agents International ("Official Travel Network")

By:_____

Title:_____

Date:_____

More Learning Through Hope (MLTH) ("Organizer")

By:_____

Title:_____

Date:_____

The most comprehensive and affordable, step-b-step sponsorship recruitment training program on the market!

Sponsorship Recruitment 101-102™
Self-Study Course

Module Eleven

SPONSORSHIP WORKBOOK

6 Learning Activities To Create Your Plan Of Action

Anthony B. Miles
With Renee Crenshaw

Sponsorship Learning Activity Package

SPONSORSHIP OPPORTUNITY PROFILE

SPONSORSHIP ACQUISITION MANAGER ACTIVITY

SPONSORSHIP LEARNING ACTIVITY PACKAGE

Class Project: 1-hour interactive sponsorship acquisition manager assignment.

Goal: To provide a practical exercise which allows the sponsorship acquisition manager to apply the knowledge gathered in this manual, toward the skill in developing a sponsorship opportunity profile.

Objective: Given your property information, develop a sponsorship opportunity profile. Explain what your property sells or proposes to sell. Describe this in detail: for example your features, audiences, budget, available sponsorship packages and facts. Here it's important to point out what separates you from your competitors' offerings and the benefits customers will derive from them.

A certain amount of imagination and creativity are required to receive the full benefit of this exercise. Now read through the Sponsorship Learning Activity Package, paying close attention to the information requested. It contains the detail needed to develop your profile. Perform each task listed below.

TASK #

_____ 1. **Site.** Enter the city and state of the sponsorship opportunity.
_____ 2. **Name.** Please list the proper title of the opportunity for which you are seeking *sponsorship.*
_____ 3. **Category.** Reflects the type of sponsorship opportunity.
_____ 4. **Date.** State the specific date or date range of your sponsorship opportunity. If its organized over a number of days you can depict this with a Schedule Chart in an addendum.
_____ 5. **Primary Contact.** The name, title, company, address, telephone, fax and e-mail address of the person responsible for sponsorship at the property. This person must be in an authoritative position to commit benefits and accept promotional consideration on behalf of the property.
_____ 6. **Attendance.** Estimate the number and categories of consumers the sponsor would be reaching by entering into a partnership with your property to participate in your proposed marketing platform.
_____ 7. **Characteristics.** Enter the characteristics of the sponsorship opportunity: budget, charity or beneficiary.
_____ 8. **Special Features:** ticketed/free, program book, food/drink or media.
_____ 9. **Sponsors.** List the key partners (your perception) with the biggest brand value. If this is the first time your opportunity has been on the market, continually update this area as you secure major sponsors. This will demonstrate to other partners your opportunity is being purchased. For on-going sponsorship opportunities list your dominant sponsors from the previous year as you start the renewal and sales process.

_____10. **Sponsor Benefits and Description.** Provide a description and list major sponsor benefits of the sponsorship opportunity.

Sponsorship Learning Activity Package

PROPERTY PLAN

SPONSORSHIP ACQUISITION TEAM ACTIVITY

SPONSORSHIP LEARNING ACTIVITY PACKAGE

Property Project: 4-hour interactive acquisition team assignment.

Goal: To provide a practical exercise which allows participants to apply the knowledge gathered in this manual, toward the skill in developing a property PLAN.

Objective: Given the 28 questions, analyze your property. Most of the information is contained in module 5, other necessary information you have already developed in module 4. A certain amount of creativity is required to receive the full benefit of this exercise. Now read through the Sponsorship Learning Activity Package, paying close attention to every question. They contain the details needed to develop your property PLAN. Once you complete your review of the package, answer each question listed.

TASK #

_____ 1.   After thoroughly reviewing the questions take a few
              minutes to discuss your property. Be certain that
              each acquisition team member has a clear understanding of the
              goals and objectives before continuing.

_____ 2.   Answer questions 1-28.

1. What is the nature of your property?

2. What phase is your property in?

A. Start-up
B. Expansion
C. Developing New Properties
D. Strategic Partners

3. What is your properties corporate structure?

A. Sole proprietor
B. Partnership
C. Corporation
D. Not-for-profit
E. Other

4. Who is your sponsorship management team?

A. Sponsorship Acquisition Manager
B. Public Relations and Communications Manager
C. Marketing & Promotions Director
D. Sponsorship Acquisition Professional
E. Licensing & Strategic Partnerships
F. Corporate Identity and Graphic Communications

5. Who is your outside consultant team?

A. Legal (intellectual properties)
B. Accounting
C. Web Site Developer
D. Event Planner
E. Sponsorship Sales

6. What is your properties unique selling advantage? (Give details on why sponsor your property).

7. What are your goals and objectives?

8. What would you like to achieve in annual sponsorship sales?

A. Year one $
B. Year two $
C. Year three $

9. How do you plan to achieve your annual sales goals?

10. What do you want for yourself personally?

11. What other sponsorship opportunities will you develop?

12. How will your sponsors receive a return on their investment?

13. What is your demographic segment profile?

A. Business Consumer

B   Individual Consumer
     Age
     Income
     Sex
     Occupation
     Family size
     Culture
     Education

14. Who is your competition?

15. How is your competition promoting its property?

16. What are your properties plans?

A. Operational Plans
B. Sponsorship Staffing Plans
C. Marketing Plans
D. Sponsor Strategy

17. How much money do you need to operate your property for two years?

18. What will the money be used for?

19. What equipment do you need?

20. Will you/do you have sponsorship sales people? If yes, please indicate their territories, commissions, and salary structures.

21. How many salespeople will you have on staff during the next 24 months?

A. Outside
B. Inside

22. When does you sponsorship fiscal year end?

23. How will you be promoting your property?

24. How much will you spend on advertising in a typical year?

25. Who are your suppliers?

26. What is your market?

27. Do you have:

A. Sponsor Testimonials
B. Endorsements
C. Consumer surveys

28. Give some background on your management team?

Sponsorship Learning Activity Package

SPONSOR ANALYSIS

SPONSORSHIP ACQUISITION MANAGER ACTIVITY

SPONSORSHIP LEARNING ACTIVITY PACKAGE

Property Project: 7-day acquisition manager assignment.

Goal: To provide a practical exercise which allows participants to apply the knowledge gathered in module 6, toward the skill in analyzing sponsors.

Objective: Given the 4 sections on the next page, analyze each sponsor. Most of the information is contained in module 6, other necessary information you gain during sponsor recruitment. Now read through the Sponsorship Learning Activity Package, paying close attention to each of the four sections. It contains the detail needed to analyze sponsors. Once you complete your review of the package, answer each question listed in the four sections.

TASK #

_____ 1.	After thoroughly reviewing the questions take a few minutes to discuss the sponsor. Be certain that you have a clear understanding of the goals and objectives before continuing.

_____ 2.	Answer the questions in sections 1-4.

#1   Nature and History of Organization

- Purpose - why was it created
- When and under what circumstances
- What type of corporation is it

#2   Sponsorship Interest and Priorities

- Scope of support-property interests
- Exclusions -what won't they sponsor?
- Geographic area of interests; exclusions
- Scope of promotional consideration - cash, product or services
- Examples of properties they have sponsored, and proposals they have turned down

#3   Sponsorship Practices and Policies

- Smallest, largest and sponsor sponsorship size
- Total annual distributions (sponsorship)
- For how many years will they sponsor the same property?
- How many requests for sponsorship do they get on average in a year?

#4   Acquisition and Evaluation Process

- What types of properties do they sponsor? Are there any categories that are excluded from consideration?
- Steps properties must go through for decision
- Do they have published guidelines?
- Deadlines - when sponsorships must be submitted for consideration
- Preferred method of inquiry: phone, meeting, letter
- Review process: who reviews?

Sponsorship Learning Activity Package

SPONSORSHIP OPPORTUNITY BROCHURE

SPONSORSHIP ACQUISITION TEAM ACTIVITY

SPONSORSHIP LEARNING ACTIVITY PACKAGE

Property Project: 4-hour interactive acquisition team assignment.

Goal: To provide a practical exercise which allows participants to apply the knowledge gathered in module 7, toward the skill in developing a Sponsorship Opportunity Brochure.

Objective: Given the three sections, prepare your marketing communications. Most of the information is contained in module 7, other necessary information you have already have developed in the previous learning activity package. A certain amount of creativity is required to receive the full benefit of this exercise. Now read through the next page, paying close attention to every question. It contains the detail needed to develop your sponsorship opportunity brochure. Once you complete your review, answer each question listed.

TASK #

_____ 1.   After thoroughly reviewing the questions take a few
minutes to discuss your property. Be certain that
each acquisition team member has a clear understanding of the
goals and objectives before continuing.

_____ 2.   Answer the questions in sections 1-3.

Sponsorship Opportunity Brochure

Company Profile of Sponsorship Opportunity **(Section 1)**

1. **Site.** Enter the city and state of the sponsorship opportunity

2. **Name.** Please list the proper title of the opportunity you are seeking *sponsorship.*

3. **Category.** Reflects the type of sponsorship opportunity

4. **Date.** State the specific date or date range of your sponsorship opportunity. If its organized over a number of days you can depict this with a schedule chart in an addendum.

5. **Primary Contact.** The name, title, company, address, telephone, fax and e-mail address of the person responsible for sponsorship at the property. This person must be in an authoritative position to commit benefits and accept promotional consideration on behalf of the property.

6. **Attendance.** Estimate the number and categories of consumers the sponsor would be reaching by entering into a partnership with your property to participate in your proposed marketing platform.

7. **Characteristics.** Enter the characteristics of the sponsorship opportunity: budget, charity or beneficiary.

8. **Special Features:** ticketed/free, program book, food/drink or media.

9. **Sponsors.** List the key partners (your perception) with the biggest brand value. If this is the first time your opportunity has been on the market, continually update this area as you secure major sponsors. This will demonstrate to other partners your opportunity is being purchased. For on-going sponsorship opportunities list your dominant sponsors from the previous year as you start the renewal and sales process.

10. **Sponsor Benefits and Description.** Provide a description and list major sponsor benefits of the sponsorship opportunity.

Marketing Opportunities & Benefits **(Section 2)**

1. What kind of marketing platform does your property provide?
2. Why sponsor your property?
3. What opportunities exist for marketers?
4. How do you help marketers leverage its sponsorship? What promotions have you created?
5. Key Benefits

Sponsorship Opportunity Analysis **(Section 3)**
1. Description
2. Audience Demographics
3. Programming
4. Hospitality Opportunities
5. Sponsorship Opportunities

Sponsorship Learning Activity Package

DEVELOPING A PROPOSAL

SPONSORSHIP ACQUISITION TEAM ACTIVITY

SPONSORSHIP LEARNING ACTIVITY PACKAGE

Class Project: 2-hour interactive group assignment

Goal: To provide a practical exercise which allows participants to apply the knowledge gathered in module 9, toward the skill in developing a sponsorship proposal.

Objective: Given the event information, develop a sponsorship proposal. Some of the information is contained in this package, other necessary information was presented during this course. A certain amount of imagination and creativity are required to receive the full benefit of this exercise. When you have a question we are here to help. Now read through the Sponsorship Learning Activity Package, paying close attention to the information sheets. They contain the details needed to develop your proposal. Once you complete your review of the package, perform each of the tasks listed below.

TASK #

_____ 1.   After thoroughly reviewing the information sheets on 289 & 290 take a few minutes to discuss this sponsorship opportunity. Be certain that each group member has a clear understanding of the of the concept and goals before continuing.

_____ 2.   Using the OAG provided, identify your salable assets. Be creative, cut imaginary deals and include those assets in your inventory.

_____ 3.   Determine the estimated value of each of the salable assets identified in the previous step.

_____ 4.   Create your sponsorship categories/or levels

_____ 5.   Using the SAI provided, perform research on several sponsors. This step will require some imagination.

_____ 6.   Select one of the sponsorship levels or categories and develop a proposal.

_____ 7.   Determine, based on your research in step 5, which sponsor you will target with your proposal.

_____ 8.   Develop your proposal.

_____ 9.   Select a representative to present your proposal.

Fresh'95

FRESH '95
OVERVIEW

Fresh'95 celebration is a one-day extravaganza for people all across our state. The celebration provides a platform for many of our area's most vibrant and talented artist. Over 10,000 Celebrities, sponsors, entertainers, professional athletes, media representatives, business leaders, TV station kids club members and the general public will converge on the county each year to participate in this mega event. This celebration is jam-packed with entertainment and activities for traveling guest and the general public during the celebration. Get ready to party - you don't want to miss this!

CELEBRITY MEET & GREET- Saturday, June 24, 1995, 10 a.m. to 12p.m., County Fairgrounds. Finally! Your chance to meet your favorite celebrities and professional athletes. You'll actually meet Lisa, Bart and Homer Simpson; The Pink Panther; and for the first time ever, The events own Fresh mascot!

FRESH '95 - FAMILY FESTIVAL- Saturday, June 24, 1995, 12 a.m. to 4 p.m., County Fairgrounds. A family event featuring entertainment, live performances, music, and of course, food! This event is geared towards kids ages 12 and under, and their families. Hurry, tickets are limited. This event is expected to sell out!

FRESH '95 - MAIN EVENT- Saturday, June 24, 1995, 6 to 11p.m., County Fairgrounds. The Fresh'95 fun continues as headline entertainers take the stage with performances aimed at young adults 13 and older. Enter the Fresh Dance Contest and win cool prizes! Hurry, tickets are limited. This event is expected to sell out!

Organizational Asset Grid (OAG) Worksheet

Organization: _____

Sponsorship Opportunity: _____

ASSETS	DESCRIPTION	VALUE
MEDIA		
Advertising Space		
Advertorial		
Balloons		
Blimps		
Billboards		
Infomercials		
News coverage		
Promotional Spots		
Public Service Announcements (PSA's)		
Remnant Space		
Remotes		
Subway & Bus Advertising		
Television Broadcasts		
Television Commercials		
Mini-Media		
Brochures		
Banners		
Signs		
Posters		
Newsletters		
Fliers		
Coupons		
Booklets		
Circulars		

(OAG) Worksheet

ASSETS	DESCRIPTION	VALUE
MINI-MEDIA (Cont.)		
Door hangers		
Gift Certificates		
Stationary		
Shelf-takers		
Bottle hangers		
Imprinted Grocery Bags		
Imprinted Register Receipts		
Targeted Media		
Customer Mailing Lists		
Postcards		
Inserts		
Catalogs		
Database Marketing		
Promotion		
Lotteries		
Sweepstakes		
Contests		
Music		
Jingles		
Packaging		
Frequent Buyer Programs		
Point of Purchase (POP)		
Point of Sale (POS)		
T-shirts		
Premiums		
Specialty Gifts		
Booths		

(OAG) Worksheet

ASSETS	DESCRIPTION	VALUE
Hospitality		
Room Nights		
Parking Validations		
Food & Beverage Credits		
Meeting Space		
Distribution Channels		
Shelf Space		
Ticket & Coupon Outlet		
Non-Media		
Logo Usage		
Personality appearances		
Celebrities		
Endorsements		
Testimonials		
Market Research		
Graphic Design Services		
Commercial Printing		
Copywriting Services		
Advertisers		
Creative & Video Production		
Advertising Sales Support		
Commercial Spot Production		
Voice Overs		

Sponsorship Levels/Category Worksheet

Organization: _____

Sponsorship Opportunity: _____

1. Which will you use?

☐ Levels   ☐ Categories   ☐ Both

2. Which levels will you offer?

☐ Title   ☐ Presenting   ☐ Co-sponsor   ☐ Sponsor   ☐ Supporters

Other

☐   ☐   ☐   ☐   ☐

3. Which categories will you offer?

☐ Automotive ☐ Bank   ☐ Packaged Goods ☐ Beverage ☐ Media

Other

☐   ☐   ☐   ☐   ☐

SPONSOR ASSET INVENTORY			
ASSETS			
MEDIA			
Advertising Space			
Advertorial			
Balloons			
Blimps			
Billboards			
Infomercials			
News coverage			
Promotional Spots			
Public Service Announcements (PSA's)			
Remnant Space			
Remotes			
Subway & Bus Advertising			
Television Broadcasts			
Television Commercials			
Mini-Media			
Brochures			
Banners			
Signs			
Posters			
Newsletters			
Fliers			
Coupons			
Booklets			

SPONSOR ASSET INVENTORY			
ASSETS			
Mini-Media (cont.)			
Circulars			
Door hangers			
Gift Certificates			
Stationary			
Shelf-takers			
Bottle hangers			
Imprinted Grocery Bags			
Imprinted Register Receipts			
Targeted Media			
Customer Mailing Lists			
Postcards			
Inserts			
Catalogs			
Database Marketing			
Promotion			
Lotteries			
Sweepstakes			
Contests			
Music			
Jingles			
Packaging			
Frequent Buyer Programs			
Point of Purchase (POP)			
Point of Sale (POS)			
T-shirts			
Premiums			

SPONSOR ASSET INVENTORY			
ASSETS			
Promotion (cont.)			
Specialty Gifts			
Booths			
Entertainment/Hospitality			
Room Nights			
Parking Validations			
Food & Beverage Credits			
Meeting Space			
Distribution Channels			
Shelf Space			
Ticket & Coupon Outlet			
Non-Media			
Logo Usage			
Personality appearances			
Celebrities			
Endorsements			
Testimonials			
Market Research			
Cash			
Graphic Design Services			
Commercial Printing			
Copywriting Services			

SPONSOR ASSET INVENTORY

ASSETS			
Non-Media (cont.)			
Advertisers			
Creative & Video Production			
Advertising Sales Support			
Commercial Spot Production			
Voice Overs			

SPONSORSHIP PRICING PLAN WORKSHEET

Sponsor:_____

Sponsorship Opportunity: _____

MEDIA   **Value:**

MINI-MEDIA: **Value:**

TARGETED MEDIA   **Value:**

PROMOTION   **Value:**

NON-MEDIA   **Value:**

Estimated Total Value $_____
Promotional Consideration Request $_____
Ratio _____ (benefit value to sponsor)

Sponsorship Proposal Blueprint

1. Sponsorship Opportunity Overview

2. Sponsor Priorities

3. Key Benefits

4. Promotional Consideration

The most comprehensive and affordable, step-b-step sponsorship recruitment training program on the market!

Sponsorship Recruitment 101-102™
Self-Study Course

Module Twelve

SAMPLE WORKSHEETS

6 Documents To Steam Line Your Sponsorship Efforts

Anthony B. Miles
With Renee Crenshaw

TARGET LIST WORKSHEET (Sponsors)		
CATEGORY	SPONSOR	BRAND

SPONSORSHIP PRICING PLAN WORKSHEET

Sponsor:_____

Sponsorship Opportunity: _____

MEDIA   **Value:**

MINI-MEDIA: **Value:**

TARGETED MEDIA   **Value:**

PROMOTION   **Value:**

NON-MEDIA   **Value:**

Estimated Total Value $_____
Promotional Consideration Request $_____
Ratio _____ (benefit value to sponsor)

Sponsor Category			
Recruitment Flow System	Sponsor	Sponsor	Sponsor
Letter of introduction & Sponsorship Opportunities Brochure			
Call for appointment			
Acceptance/Rejection			
Thank you to Rejection			
Add to Mailing List			
Date of Appointment			
Thank you following appointment			
Research Sales Overlays			
Proposal Sent (with attachment)			
Proposal copy for site visit			
Thank you Letter following Appointment			
Date of Decision Making			
Rejected/Accepted			
Thank You Letter			
Amount Received			
Amount Requested			

SPONSOR ASSET INVENTORY			
ASSETS			
MEDIA			
Advertising Space			
Advertorial			
Balloons			
Blimps			
Billboards			
Infomercials			
News coverage			
Promotional Spots			
Public Service Announcements (PSA's)			
Remnant Space			
Remotes			
Subway & Bus Advertising			
Television Broadcasts			
Television Commercials			
Mini-Media			
Brochures			
Banners			
Signs			
Posters			
Newsletters			
Fliers			
Coupons			
Booklets			

SPONSOR ASSET INVENTORY			
ASSETS			
Mini-Media (cont.)			
Circulars			
Door hangers			
Gift Certificates			
Stationary			
Shelf-takers			
Bottle hangers			
Imprinted Grocery Bags			
Imprinted Register Receipts			
Targeted Media			
Customer Mailing Lists			
Postcards			
Inserts			
Catalogs			
Database Marketing			
Promotion			
Lotteries			
Sweepstakes			
Contests			
Music			
Jingles			
Packaging			
Frequent Buyer Programs			
Point of Purchase (POP)			
Point of Sale (POS)			
T-shirts			
Premiums			

SPONSOR ASSET INVENTORY			
ASSETS			
Promotion (cont.)			
Specialty Gifts			
Booths			
Entertainment/Hospitality			
Room Nights			
Parking Validations			
Food & Beverage Credits			
Meeting Space			
Distribution Channels			
Shelf Space			
Ticket & Coupon Outlet			
Non-Media			
Logo Usage			
Personality appearances			
Celebrities			
Endorsements			
Testimonials			
Market Research			
Cash			
Graphic Design Services			
Commercial Printing			
Copywriting Services			

SPONSOR ASSET INVENTORY			
ASSETS			
Non-Media (cont.)			
Advertisers			
Creative & Video Production			
Advertising Sales Support			
Commercial Spot Production			
Voice Overs			

Organizational Asset Grid (OAG) Worksheet

Organization: _____

Sponsorship Opportunity: _____

ASSETS	DESCRIPTION	VALUE
MEDIA		
Advertising Space		
Advertorial		
Balloons		
Blimps		
Billboards		
Infomercials		
News coverage		
Promotional Spots		
Public Service Announcements (PSA's)		
Remnant Space		
Remotes		
Subway & Bus Advertising		
Television Broadcasts		
Television Commercials		
Mini-Media		
Brochures		
Banners		
Signs		
Posters		
Newsletters		
Fliers		
Coupons		
Booklets		
Circulars		

(OAG) Worksheet

ASSETS	DESCRIPTION	VALUE
MINI-MEDIA (Cont.)		
Door hangers		
Gift Certificates		
Stationary		
Shelf-takers		
Bottle hangers		
Imprinted Grocery Bags		
Imprinted Register Receipts		
Targeted Media		
Customer Mailing Lists		
Postcards		
Inserts		
Catalogs		
Database Marketing		
Promotion		
Lotteries		
Sweepstakes		
Contests		
Music		
Jingles		
Packaging		
Frequent Buyer Programs		
Point of Purchase (POP)		
Point of Sale (POS)		
T-shirts		
Premiums		
Specialty Gifts		
Booths		

(OAG) Worksheet

ASSETS	DESCRIPTION	VALUE
Hospitality		
Room Nights		
Parking Validations		
Food & Beverage Credits		
Meeting Space		
Distribution Channels		
Shelf Space		
Ticket & Coupon Outlet		
Non-Media		
Logo Usage		
Personality appearances		
Celebrities		
Endorsements		
Testimonials		
Market Research		
Graphic Design Services		
Commercial Printing		
Copywriting Services		
Advertisers		
Creative & Video Production		
Advertising Sales Support		
Commercial Spot Production		
Voice Overs		

Sponsorship Levels/Category
Worksheet

Organization: _____

Sponsorship Opportunity: _____

1. Which will you use?

☐ Levels   ☐ Categories   ☐ Both

2. Which levels will you offer?

☐ Title   ☐ Presenting   ☐ Co-sponsor   ☐ Sponsor   ☐ Supporters

Other
☐   ☐   ☐   ☐   ☐

3. Which categories will you offer?

☐Automotive ☐ Bank   ☐Packaged Goods ☐Beverage ☐ Media

Other
☐   ☐   ☐   ☐   ☐

The most comprehensive and affordable, step-b-step sponsorship recruitment training program on the market!

Sponsorship Recruitment 101-102™
Self-Study Course

Module Thirteen

SPONSORSHIP RESOURCES

6 Powerful Tools To Increase Your Sponsorship Funding

Anthony B. Miles

With Renee Crenshaw

Miles International welcomes You to the...

US Sponsorship Resource Center

"The world's largest one-stop-shop for all your sponsorship needs"

We have designed this resource center for not-for-profit professionals of all denominations worldwide to help with their sponsorship recruitment efforts.

We work to enhance profitability, improve your properties packaging, grow your sponsorship funding base, and maximize sponsorship sales through effective, client-centered marketing strategies.

3 Powerful Resource tools to Increase Your Sponsorships Efforts:

8-week Fast Track Sponsorship Course – Get More Sponsorship Dollars Than You Thought Possible – With the Interactive Sponsorship Course That's So Powerful, it Guarantees Your Success!

1 1/2 day Regional Sponsorship Seminar – Discover How-to Flood Your Programs With A Steady Stream of Sponsorship Dollars More Quickly and Easily Than You Ever Thought Possible!

6-month Personalized Sponsorship Instruction & Coaching Program – "Here's How You Can Quickly and Easily Get Anthony To Help You Build A Six Figure Sponsorship Recruitment Program...*Without* Breaking the Bank!"

Miles International
5012 Erringer Place
Philadelphia, PA 19144
215-843-0571
215-843-0572 (FAX)
E-mail: **ussrc@milesinternational.org**

<u>8-week Fast Track Sponsorship Course</u>

Get More Sponsorship Dollars Than You Thought Possible – With the Interactive Sponsorship Course that's so powerful, it Guarantees Your Success!

Learn all the secrets of building your very own super successful sponsorship program -- at a Special Introductory Price that's so good, we can only offer it to a limited number of participants!

Dear Not-for-profit Executive,

Have you ever wondered why some organizations seem to get sponsorships almost effortlessly...while you always seem to be struggling to find even the minimal funding you need to keep your programs afloat?

Well, if you think there must be a secret to getting sponsorship dollars, you're absolutely right. But finding out those secrets isn't as difficult as you might think. The fact is, in just eight short weeks you can...

Learn all the secrets to getting sponsorship dollars pouring in – direct from a sponsorship expert so well known throughout the industry for his success that he's heralded as "The Money Man" !

How?

"The Money Man," Anthony B. Miles, leading authority on not-for-profit sponsorship and producer of the most-attended not-for-profit seminar of all time, has created the ultimate way to learn the secrets of creating your own incredibly successful sponsorship program.

It's called *the 8-Week Fast Track Sponsorship Course* — and it's absolutely the most efficient, powerful way ever offered to learn from the master of successful sponsorships!

Much more than a simple collection of tapes or manuals, *the 8-Week Fast Track Sponsorship Course* is an interactive 8-week accelerated self-study program that guides you, step-by-step, through everything you need to know to get the most sponsorship dollars for your organization as quickly as possible.

> *"Anthony's unbelievable! He coached me, and I have raised over $117,000 for our ministry. His program really works."*
> *--Cheryl Toddman,*
> *Dir. of Corporate Sponsorships,*
> *St. Paul Baptist Church*

Learning with *The 8-week Fast Track Sponsorship Course* couldn't be easier. It's been specifically designed to offer maximum results in minimum time. At the start of each week, you simply read over the comprehensive lesson, which unveils Anthony's amazing arsenal of techniques and tips. Then you complete the homework assigned with that lesson.

But here's where the course really stands out from other sponsorship learning programs.

Every time you complete an assignment, it will be reviewed, critiqued and evaluated by "The Money Man," Anthony B. Miles, himself. This is a tremendous value — **Anthony charges $350.00 per hour for consulting. But you get this guidance FREE when you sign up for the program (that's a $2,800 value!).**

Each week for 8 weeks, you simply go through each lesson in a logical, step-by-step fashion, completing the assignments as you go. By the time you have completed the course, you'll be fully armed with all of the techniques, strategies and secrets you need to recruit sponsors right away.

And each step along the way, Anthony will be there with you, evaluating your ideas, identifying sponsors, critiquing your proposals, encouraging you along, fine-tuning your sponsorship sales strategy, and giving you the push you need to really get going.

Here's A Quick Overview of the Amazing Information you'll discover inside the 8-Week Fast Track Sponsorship Course:

Understanding the Game of Sponsorship. In the first week, you'll be introduced to the "game" of sponsorships... and how to play to win!

Property Analysis. In the second week, you move on to the art of analyzing your property to present the best possible scenario to sponsors you're targeting.

Sponsorship Blueprint Design. The blueprint is absolutely essential to get the sponsorship dollars you need! Anthony guides you through the process and offers you his invaluable tips for creating the ultimate blueprint for success.

Sponsor Analysis. How do you identify the sponsors most likely to give you the funding you need? Anthony uncovers the secrets to successfully analyzing potential sponsors...keeping you from targeting unlikely sponsors and saving you untold hours of your valuable time.

Sponsorship Packaging. Putting together a wining proposal is what really seals the deal. Get a firsthand look at Anthony's winning strategies!

...And much, much more! The course also covers Anthony's insider secrets about sponsorship recruitment, proposal development, and an in-depth look at sponsorship in action. Plus his systematic approach, with worksheets, to give you the knowledge to identify and price salable assets, formulate a budget, and create your sponsorship plan.

In fact, there's so much practical, usable, eye-opening information in this course that we couldn't possibly cover it all here.

We've seen sponsorship consultants charging as much as $7,000 or more for advice that isn't as in-depth and practical as Anthony's. So you see why it really makes sense to sign up for *the 8-week Fast Track Sponsorship Course* and get all the insider's secrets you'll need -- for just a fraction of the price.

The 8-week Fast Track Sponsorship Course will normally be offered for the remarkably affordable price of $1,595 -- a terrific investment, especially when you consider the thousands of dollars in free one-on-one, personalized coaching you'll be receiving directly from Anthony himself.

Even Better Price With Our Introductory Special Offer -- IF You Sign Up Right Away!

Even Better Offer: Right now, *the 8-week Fast Track Sponsorship Course* -- and over $2,800 worth of personal coaching — can be yours for a limited-time only price of just $1,185!

This special price is available exclusively to the first 100 not-for-profits. After that, it goes back up to the regular price (still an amazing bargain, considering how much Anthony usually charges per hour).

I think you'll agree that we could have asked for much more -- after all, this course gives you insider secrets you won't find anywhere else, and will help you obtain thousands of dollars in sponsorships. This is the kind of investment that can pay for itself many, many times over.

And ordering is completely risk-free. In fact, we're about to offer you an exceptionally generous and outright daring guarantee...

Our "No-Quibbles, Right-Upfront, Double-Your-Money-Back" Guarantee

Our guarantee: After purchasing *the 8-week Fast Track Sponsorship Course*, if you've actively used and followed our Systems Approach for 12 months after course completion and have not secured at least $10,000 in cash, products or services, we'll give you double your money back.

We'd be completely nuts to offer such an amazing guarantee if we didn't believe wholeheartedly that this course would offer you returns many, many times over.

One Important Qualification Before You Sign Up:

Before you sign up for *the 8-week Fast Track Sponsorship Course*, you have to promise that you will follow the techniques Anthony shares with you to the letter. You must be willing to rigorously adhere to actually doing all the assignments and following Anthony's advice -- or there's really no point to taking the course. **Nobody gets in without this assurance.**

We fully expect the response to this announcement to be huge, so don't wait another minute if you'd like to get in on this! Every minute that passes drastically increases the chance of your slot being taken by another not-for-profit. Once our limited number of positions are filled, it's over -- and we'd hate to see you miss out.

Reserve your space in *the 8-week Fast Track Sponsorship Course* now!!

www.ussponsorshipresourcecenter.com

Miles International
P.O. Box 44607
Philadelphia, PA 19144
215-843-0571
215-843-0572 (FAX)
E-mail: **ussrc@milesinternational.org**

In Just 1 _ days, you can Discover

How to Flood Your Programs With A Steady Stream of Sponsorship Dollars More Quickly and Easily

Than You Thought Possible!

Overnight, you'll possess all the secrets to getting the sponsorship dollars you need — thanks to an incredible 1 _ day regional seminar open only to a limited number of participants.

Dear Not-for-profit Executive,

If you've been wondering how other people get hold of the sponsorship dollars that always seem to slip through your fingers, we have incredibly exciting and rare opportunity for you.

Anthony B. Miles, the world's leading authority on not-for-profit Corporate Sponsorships and Promotional Activities, is hosting a seminar — **his** US Nonprofit Sponsorship Seminar — **in your area for 1 _ days only. Here's your chance to secure your place in this invaluable seminar** — **and learn for yourself the secrets to securing thousands in cash, products and services!**

US Nonprofit Sponsorship Seminar is an absolutely essential resource for anyone in the not-for-profit industry. This enlightening 1 _ day training program has the power to transform both new and experienced not-for-profit executives into "sponsorship pros" overnight.

In this seminar, Anthony reveals all of the remarkable tricks, strategies, and methods he uses to secure a stream of sponsorship dollars for not-for-profits throughout the U.S.

Anthony receives requests for this type of training all the time. People are pleading for Anthony to reveal everything he does to secure sponsorship funding. Now, he's ready to put on this amazing "Money-Magician-Unveils-The-Secrets-Behind-Successful-Sponsorship-Funding" seminar in your area for 1 _ days only.

In this seminar, Anthony shares his eye-opening **8-step** system that teaches not-for-profits of any denomination how to effectively secure sponsors for programs, conferences, fundraising and special events. Over 5,000 not-for-profits throughout North America have gotten the competitive edge by using Anthony's Systematic Approach. And now it's available to you at a fraction of the cost at this limited-time seminar.

Seminar participants will have the rare opportunity to hear Anthony live — and the chance to network with other not-for-profits who are attending.

Here's a little insight into the tremendous power and remarkable value of the strategies and tips Anthony teaches and discusses in this Seminar Package. In **US Sponsorship Seminar,** you'll learn how to:

● **Speak** the sponsorship language to sound like an expert — and get people behind your events.

• **Determine** how much sponsorship you can realistically raise, saving yourself untold hours of wasted effort...so you can focus on only the most promising sources of funds.

• **Create** a functional plan that will get you the sponsorship funds you need.

• **Handpick** the right sponsorship categories to fund your property.

• **Perform** an assessment to identify and price what you have to offer sponsors...making it much more likely that they'll give you what you ask for.

• **Design** powerful marketing communications that get sponsors to tell you exactly what they want...so you can give it to them and close the deal.

• **Work up** customized sponsorship proposals that your sponsors simply can't refuse.

• **Deliver** persuasive presentations that connect with a sponsor's product or service.

You'll leave this seminar MUCH more skilled and MUCH better equipped to achieve the absolute maximum possible results in any sponsorship situation. This seminar offers the skills and techniques that can quite literally change you and the way you approach sponsorship opportunities.

Incredibly, This Seminar Is Open To You For Considerably Less Than You Would Normally Have To Pay Anthony For His Advice.

If you act now to reserve your space in this seminar (we expect standing-room-only attendance), you'll get all of Anthony's advice for the special, limited-time price of only $249. Top executives pay Anthony $4,500 for 1 _ days of his advice, so you can see how invaluable this seminar is.

But don't take our word for it - here are just a few of the rave reviews for Anthony's Sponsorship guidance:

"...a valuable tool for securing more funds in this day and age of shrinking government support. Excellent!"
--**Marcia S. Breiter,** *Program Coordinator, City of Miami*

"...really makes you focus on sponsor benefits and gets the creative juices flowing."
--**Alastair Lyall,** *Special Events Coordinator, City of Avon*

"I've increased my knowledge by 100%."
--**John Jackson,** *Director, St. Cloud Parks & Recreation*

Don't miss your chance to get into this one-time-only, no holds barred, every tip and technique revealed, 1 _ day seminar.

This seminar is absolutely "atomic"!

Who should attend?

People who are responsible for securing sponsorship funding for age care facilities, arts/cultural groups, associations, charities, environmental groups, educational bodies, hospitals, disability foundations, international aid societies, local government, philanthropic organizations, professional societies, religious groups, service clubs, major sporting bodies, trade associations, welfare agencies and youth affairs should ABSOLUTELY attend this invaluable seminar.

WARNING: This seminar is reserved ONLY for people who are completely serious about learning world-class, powerful and very time-efficient sponsorship techniques.

This kind of seminar is definitely not for everyone. You really should NOT attend if you're not serious about getting the funding your programs need.

About the Instructor

Anthony "The Money Man" Miles is the world's leading authority on not-for-profit Corporate Sponsorships and Promotional Activities. His seminars and manuals have made a profound impact on thousands of not-for-profits throughout North America...from the American Red Cross...to Universities...to Sports Commissions...to Symphonies...to Parks & Recreation...to Association Executives...to Professional Golf...and cities all over the United States.

Anthony is the author of **Sponsorship Recruitment 101-102.** He is the producer of the best selling not-for-profit sponsorship seminar of all time, Sponsorship Recruitment 101-102. He is the recipient of over 50 community service, business and leadership awards.

Anthony has earned his professional reputation the right way, though dedication, customer satisfaction and just plan hard work. He has dedicated his life to helping not-for-profits meet their funding objectives. This passion has earned him the nickname **"The Money Man."** His ability to electrify a crowd with his presence -- as well as his cutting-edge strategies -- have catapulted him into a class of his own.

Simply put, Anthony is the Michael Jordan of the not-for-profit sponsorship world.

Don't Miss Out!

This will be your only chance to obtain a first hand perspective on the hottest trends, freshest thinking and leading opportunities to secure sponsorship funding for you organization. We urge you to enroll today to ensure your place.

Here's How You Get Started

If you're SERIOUS about arming yourself with Anthony's techniques and skills, then we're sure you'll agree: the investment for this Sponsorship Seminar is quite small indeed. The bottom line is simple: if you want to become an overnight sponsorship pro, securing floods of cash and services for your organization at will...with the ability to do it quickly and efficiently... making sure your programs receive the dollars they deserve...you'll be sure NOT to miss this amazing one-time opportunity.

Right now, you can make sure your space at the **US Nonprofit Sponsorship Seminar** isn't snatched up by someone else. Remember, we're expecting standing-room-only crowds, and space is very limited, so to be absolutely sure your space is held for you, choose your seminar and reserve your space today.

Simply choose the seminar that's most convenient for you to attend, then **click the button below to reserve your space today. Don't put it off until tomorrow...only to find out it's too late!!!**

2004 Training Locations and Dates
- **East – Philadelphia, PA/September 9-10, 2004**
- **North – Chicago, IL/October 7-8, 2004**
- **South - Miami, FL/November 11-12, 2004**
- **West – Phoenix, AZ/December 2-3, 2004**

www.ussponsorshipresourcecenter.com

Miles International
5012 Erringer Place
Philadelphia, PA 19144
215-843-0571
215-843-0572 (FAX)
E-mail: **ussrc@milesinternational.org**

"Anthony's Unbelievable, he coached me and I have raised over $117,000 for our ministry. His program really works."
—Cheryl Toddman, Dir. of Corporate Sponsorships, St. Paul Community Baptist Church,

Stop Putting Up With lack of funding...
Here's How You Can Quickly and Easily Get Anthony To Help You Build A Six Figure Sponsorship Recruitment Program...<u>Without</u> Breaking the Bank!

Dear Not-for-Profit Executive,

How much is sponsorship funding worth to your organization? Suppose you could achieve stellar results and get all the sponsors you need. Imagine...hundred of thousands of dollars in cash, products or services every year.

Sounds too good to be true?

Well, it isn't if you have Anthony on your team. Think about it. Normally it would be next to impossible to add a sponsorship expert such as Anthony to your staff without breaking the bank. But now you can add Anthony to your sponsorship mix for the next 6-months for virtually pennies.

Stop Risking Your Valuable Time, Effort, and Money on Ineffective Sponsorship Recruitment — Put Anthony on Your Team and Watch Your Sales Soar

It could take you years and can cost you a small fortune to figure out just the right combinations that make your sponsorship program work.

But instead of knocking yourself out trying to come up with just the wining formula, you can now tap Anthony with this new sponsorship resource called:

"The 6-month Personalized Sponsorship

Instruction & Coaching Program"

At last! All the support you ever needed is here.

I know you're probably still skeptical and a bit on the conservative side, but think about this - if you keep doing the same things over and over again - you'll only succeed in getting the same results. That's why I want to let try out my proven sponsorship system - <u>completely and totally risk-free</u>! (I'll tell you about my unique guarantee in a moment.)

Here's how it works!

You get 18 sessions with Anthony, 3-hours each month for 6-months.

♣ Use your hour to ask Anthony sponsorship questions and get no-holds-barred answers.

♣ Use it to have Anthony tune up your property profile, sales letter, or sponsorship marketing piece.

♣ Use your hour to identify sponsorship prospects.

♣ Perhaps Anthony could help critique your sponsorship proposal or walk through a sponsorship pitch making constructive suggestions.

♣ Or use it for anything else for which you need an a seasoned sponsorship pro like Anthony at your side.

Okay, So What's the Cost for This Incredible Resource?

Well, realize that this personal instruction & coaching program could easily sell for tens of thousands of dollars. In fact if you asked a top expert, like myself, to create your sponsorship packages for you, you'd be charged in the neighborhood of $7,000 to $10,000, not including graphics charges.

But I'm not going to charge you anywhere near that amount or even my minimum project price. **In fact, your total investment for** the 6-month Personalized Sponsorship Instruction & Coaching Program **is only** $3,240

So what's the catch? Why am I practically giving this resource away?

Well, it's really quite simple. I need the money. I trying to purchase 10 homes fix them up and make them available to low income families.

[1] FREE Bonus for Ordering Within the next 30 days

Free Bonus Gift #1: Private 1-day On-site Sponsorship Training & Consulting Session. Anthony will spend a full day at your site training your board, leadership and staff members. Anthony supplies the time you pick-up the expenses (A $5,000 value).

This free bonus more than exceeds your investment in the coaching program -- but they're all yours absolutely free when you order **within the next 30 days.**

100% Risk-Free Guarantee:

Your success in using the 6-month Personalized Instruction & Coaching Program is completely guaranteed. In fact, here's my 100% Better-Than-Risk-Free-Take-it-To-The-Bank Guarantee:

After purchasing *the 6-month Coaching Program*, if you've actively used and followed our Systems Approach for 12 months after course completion and have not secured at least $15,000 in cash, products or services, we'll give you your money back.

Is that fair or what?

That means you can try out our personalized sponsorship instruction & coaching program at my risk, while you see if they work for you or not. And if they don't produce, I honestly want you to ask for your money back. And I'll let you keep the free bonus gifts as my way of thanking you for giving my coaching program a try.

There is absolutely no risk, whatsoever on your part. The burden to deliver is entirely on me. If you don't produce immediate profits using my instruction & coaching then I'm the loser, not you.

Look at it this way -- $3,240 is really a painless drop in the bucket compared to the money you're going to waste on ineffective sponsorship recruitment this year. That's why...

**You Really Can't Afford Not To Invest In
our Personalized Sponsorship Instruction & Coaching Program!**

We fully expect the response to this announcement to be huge, so don't wait another minute if you'd like to get in on this! Every minute that passes drastically increases the chance of your slot being taken by another not-for-profit. Once our limited number of positions is filled, it's over -- and we'd hate to see you miss out.

Reserve your space today! Get ready for big results.

www.ussponsorshipresourcecenter.com

Miles International
5012 Erringer Place
Philadelphia, PA 19144
215-843-0571
215-843-0572 (FAX)
E-mail: **ussrc@milesinternational.org**